Can We Trust the Bible on the Historical Jesus?

Can We Trust the Bible on the Historical Jesus?

BART D. EHRMAN
CRAIG A. EVANS
AND
ROBERT B. STEWART

© 2020 Westminster John Knox Press

First edition
Published by Westminster John Knox Press
Louisville, Kentucky

20 21 22 23 24 25 26 27 28 29—10 9 8 7 6 5 4 3 2 1

All rights reserved. No part of this book may be reproduced or transmitted in any form or by any means, electronic or mechanical, including photocopying, recording, or by any information storage or retrieval system, without permission in writing from the publisher. For information, address Westminster John Knox Press, 100 Witherspoon Street, Louisville, Kentucky 40202-1396. Or contact us online at www.wjkbooks.com.

Scripture quotations from the NRSV are from the New Revised Standard Version of the Bible, copyright © 1989 by the Division of Christian Education of the National Council of the Churches of Christ in the U.S.A., and are used by permission. In this book, Scripture may be paraphrased or summarized.

Book design by Drew Stevens
Cover design by Marc Whitaker / MTWdesign.net

Library of Congress Cataloging-in-Publication Data
Names: Ehrman, Bart D., author. | Evans, Craig A., author. | Stewart, Robert B., 1957– author.
Title: Can we trust the Bible on the historical Jesus? / Bart D. Ehrman, Craig A. Evans and Robert B. Stewart.
Description: First edition. | Louisville, Kentucky : WJK, Westminster John Knox Press, 2020. | Includes bibliographical references and index. | Summary: "This book features a debate between two great Bible scholars, Bart Ehrman and Craig Evans, about the New Testament as a reliable source on the historical Jesus and what constitutes "history." This debate, along with Robert Stewart's introductory framework, make this book an excellent primer to the study of the historical Jesus"— Provided by publisher.
Identifiers: LCCN 2020024009 (print) | LCCN 2020024010 (ebook) | ISBN 9780664265854 (paperback) | ISBN 9781646980017 (ebook)
Subjects: LCSH: Jesus Christ—Historicity. | Bible. New Testament—Evidences, authority, etc.
Classification: LCC BT303.2 .E465 2020 (print) | LCC BT303.2 (ebook) | DDC 232.9/08—dc23
LC record available at https://lccn.loc.gov/2020024009
LC ebook record available at https://lccn.loc.gov/2020024010

Most Westminster John Knox Press books are available at special quantity discounts when purchased in bulk by corporations, organizations, and special-interest groups. For more information, please email SpecialSales@wjkbooks.com.

*To our respective colleagues in
the School of Christian Thought, Houston Baptist University;
the Department of Religious Studies at the University
of North Carolina at Chapel Hill; and the Theological
and Historical Division, New Orleans Baptist Theological Seminary*

The Bible also cannot be trusted as a historical source. It may provide great literature, and you may choose to use it for your theological beliefs, but it is not historically accurate.
—Bart Ehrman

Can we trust what the New Testament says about the historical Jesus? In a word, yes. If I did not trust what the New Testament says about Jesus, then it would not be easy to be a Christian.
—Craig Evans

The Gospels may be more than historical documents *in that they clearly are meant to convey a theological message as well as a historical record, but they cannot be* less than historical documents.
—Robert Stewart

Contents

Acknowledgments	ix
Abbreviations	xi
Introduction: History, Historians, and Trusting Historical Texts *Robert B. Stewart*	1
History and Historians	1
Trusting Historical Texts	12
What's at Stake?	18
Can We Trust the Bible on the Historical Jesus? *A Dialogue between Bart D. Ehrman and Craig A. Evans*	21
Bart Ehrman: Opening Statement	21
Craig Evans: Opening Statement	34
Bart Ehrman: Response	53
Craig Evans: Response	57
Bart Ehrman: Conclusion	60
Craig Evans: Conclusion	62
Questions and Answers	65
The State of the Quest for the Historical Jesus *Robert B. Stewart*	75
Further Reading *Robert B. Stewart*	85
Index	97

Acknowledgments

Thanking others in print is always an occasion for anxiety because of the fear that some who deserve a word of appreciation will be overlooked through human error. But many deserve to be publicly thanked, and even praised, so we must go on. The dialogue that is featured in this book came from the seventh Greer-Heard Point-Counterpoint Forum. The Greer-Heard Forum was a five-year pilot project of New Orleans Baptist Theological Seminary (NOBTS) that began in 2005. The Forum was made possible by a generous gift from donors Bill and Carolyn Greer Heard; the forum was named in honor of their parents.

Apparently they were pleased with the results from the five-year trial period because in total there were fourteen Greer-Heard dialogues. So, first of all, we must thank Bill and Carolyn Heard for their passion to have a forum where leading scholars can dialogue about important issues in faith and culture in a collegial manner and on a balanced playing field. Without them the Greer-Heard Point-Counterpoint Forum in Faith and Culture would be a dream rather than a reality.

The event would never have come off successfully without the efforts of J. P. Cox and his staff at the Providence Learning Center of NOBTS. Vanee Daure and the media staff of NOBTS must also be thanked for recording it in both audio and video formats.

The initial transcription of the dialogue was done by Robert Stewart's research assistant, Raphael Forrer. He deserves a word of thanks not only for the transcription but also for carrying out other tasks related to the project flawlessly and with enthusiasm. Thanks to Micah Chung for creating the index. Bryan

Shuler and Marissa Elias also need to be thanked for their assistance with details of the project in its final stages.

We very much appreciate Daniel Braden at Westminster John Knox for his interest in publishing this volume as well as his enthusiasm for fair-minded, respectful dialogue on important issues. Additionally, he was always timely in responding to questions and a source of much good advice and encouragement.

As always, our wives and family members must be thanked; they are consistent sources of support. In addition, we are grateful for the academic encouragement we receive from our colleagues in our fields at our respective schools. It is to them that we dedicate this book.

Abbreviations

ABRL	Anchor Bible Reference Library
AD	*anno Domini*
AsJT	*Asia Journal of Theology*
BAR	*Biblical Archaeology Review*
BBR	*Bulletin for Biblical Research*
BC	before Christ
BTB	*Biblical Theology Bulletin*
ca. (or c.)	circa, approximately
CBQ	*Catholic Biblical Quarterly*
CE	Common Era
Co.	Company
ed(s).	editor(s), edited by, edition
esp.	especially
et al.	*et alii*, and others
frag.	fragment
i.e.	*id est*, that is
HistTh	*History and Theory*
HTR	*Harvard Theological Review*
HUCA	*Hebrew Union College Annual*
ICC	International Critical Commentary
JBL	*Journal of Biblical Literature*
JETS	*Journal of the Evangelical Theological Society*
JSHJ	*Journal for the Study of the Historical Jesus*

JSNTSup	Journal for the Study of the New Testament Supplement Series
JTS	*Journal of Theological Studies*
LCL	Loeb Classical Library
LNTS	The Library of New Testament Studies
ms(s).	manuscript(s)
NOBTS	New Orleans Baptist Theological Seminary
NTTS	New Testament Tools and Studies
NTTSD	New Testament Tools, Studies, and Documents
𝔓	papyrus or papyri, numbered
p(p).	page(s)
SBL	Society of Biblical Literature
SBLRBS	Society of Biblical Literature Resources for Biblical Study
SBLTT	Society of Biblical Literature Texts and Translations
SBT	Studies in Biblical Theology
SHT	Studies in Historical Theology
SJT	*Scottish Journal of Theology*
SNTSMS	Society for New Testament Studies Monograph Series
trans.	translator, translated by
TSJTSA	Texts and Studies of the Jewish Theological Seminary of America
TTKi	*Tidsskrift for Teologi og Kirke*
U.S.	United States of America
WUNT	Wissenschaftliche Untersuchungen zum Neuen Testament

Introduction

History, Historians, and Trusting Historical Texts

ROBERT B. STEWART

HISTORY AND HISTORIANS

"What is history and what is the role of the historian?" I regularly pose that question to my students and colleagues. I never cease to be amazed at how often history majors and even working historians have not reflected critically on the nature of their task. In no way is this introduction intended to be the definitive answer to either of these questions; instead, I'm hoping that it will be a helpful step toward such an answer and help the reader to better appreciate the Ehrman-vs.-Evans debate that follows.

History is a retelling of significant events that happened in the past. Simply put, historians tell stories about the past. This means that we must distinguish between history as an *event* in the past (History-E) and history as what is *written* about select events in the past (History-W). With responsible historians, the event is the origin of the story, chronological ground zero, if you will. Ancient historians writing on an event (or a person) were reporting on that event (or person); in so doing they were crafting the history that is available to us today.

History is necessarily an interpretive task. One cannot separate history from hermeneutics. Before one can make a historical judgment related to a text, one must first engage in a hermeneutical quest for meaning. The first step in reading any text is to ask what it means, what it intends to communicate to its readers. Even after the initial hermeneutical work is done, more hermeneutical work may be required. John Dominic Crossan helpfully distinguishes between the *mode* of the resurrection and the *meaning* of the resurrection. "Mode" has to do with whether language is to be taken literally or historically (Jesus was a peasant from Nazareth) or metaphorically (Jesus is the Lamb of God). "Meaning" has to do with the implications of a text (whether taken literally/historically or metaphorically).[1]

History is also the interpretation of human actions, in particular the interpretation of the *motivations* of significant figures for choosing to act as they did, and *what they hoped to achieve* through such actions. Though some history involves the retelling of things like natural disasters—such as tornados and earthquakes, which can at one level be explained scientifically—most history focuses upon the individual persons whose choices or opinions were decisive at crucial moments in wars, politics, the economy, social movements, or scientific breakthroughs (though obviously historians also write on more mundane subjects like entertainment or sports). For this reason historians sometimes write anthropomorphically, such as "Hitler invaded Poland" or "Lincoln ended slavery." On the other hand, sometimes individual choices are institutionalized such that historians speak in metonymy, as in "the White House announced today that the meeting is off."

History proceeds on the basis of inferences. Actions are public, but thoughts are private. Therefore historians must *infer* what motivates a person to act and what the person was attempting to achieve through the act being studied. Sometimes historical figures, or earlier historians writing about them, will state their reasons for acting, but even then historians must infer whether

---

1. John Dominic Crossan, "Appendix: Bodily-Resurrection Faith," in *The Resurrection of Jesus: John Dominic Crossan and N. T. Wright in Dialogue*, ed. Robert B. Stewart (Minneapolis: Fortress Press, 2006), 171–73, 184.

to believe those persons or not. Even when historical figures are truthful, there may still be more to the story than they admit (or sometimes even realize themselves). Simply put, the figures about whom historians write have their own agendas; thus historians need to recognize such agendas and critically interpret what those persons say.

History is never comprehensive. This is so for two primary reasons. First, much of the past is inaccessible to historians. Second, historians make judgment calls as to what to include and what to leave out of the story that they are (re)telling about the past because some matters are significant and others are not. For instance, I don't care whether presidential candidates prefer Bach or Beethoven, but I do care whether they get their ethics from *Mein Kampf* or the Sermon on the Mount. Because historians make these judgments, *history in some sense is derivative.* This means three things. First, historians are reading history as well as writing it. Because we moderns don't have direct observational access to the past, historians today cite historians of the past as "sources" of information or data—who often get their history from earlier historians. Second, historians are the gatekeepers to the past. Third, sometimes ancient historians do not address the issues that most concern us. This should not surprise us: they weren't writing to us!

Because historians are the gatekeepers, we must be aware not only of the agendas of historical figures but also of the agendas of the historians writing about them. For example, both Ann Coulter[2] and George Stephanopoulos[3] have written books about the Clinton White House. Both have agendas; their agendas are not remotely similar. In the same way, one should understand the perspectives of ancient historians and modern historians writing about the ancient world. In fact, knowledge of the agenda of a historical figure may increase the historian's ability to know the truth. Consider the criterion of embarrassment, according to which any pericope including elements that

---

2. Ann Coulter, *High Crimes and Misdemeanors: The Case against Bill Clinton* (Washington, DC: Regnery Publishing, 1998).
3. George Stephanopoulos, *All Too Human: A Political Education* (Boston: Little, Brown & Co., 1999).

could be embarrassing to the author or the author's group is presumed to be true because otherwise the author would be disinclined to record it. Knowing the author's agenda seems to be required if one is to use this criterion effectively.

This is not to deny that there is a truth to matters of the past, or to mean that all historical writing is simply a matter of perspective. History is, of course, a matter of perspective, but not merely a matter of perspective. For instance, either Nixon knew about the Watergate cover-up or he did not. Either Jesus was buried after he was crucified or he was not. The perspectival nature of history does nothing to mitigate the laws of non-contradiction and excluded middle.

Sometimes an agenda actually aids the historian in getting at the truth. A historian who is passionately interested in finding the truth may pursue the truth more diligently than one who is emotionally detached. On other occasions an agenda can blind historians in their search for truth.

Historical investigation is somewhat analogous to scientific investigation. In some ways the task of the New Testament historian is like that of the theoretical scientist. Neither one has direct access to the event or events that they are concerned to understand. The Jesus scholar of today can no more get back to the first century than the cosmologist can get back to the big bang. Nevertheless, both scholars have reason to think that they can come to know a significant amount about the past.

Neither the scientist nor the historian should be under the illusion that they can "prove" that their view is the correct view, although they can make cogent arguments in favor of their conclusions. Cosmologist Sean Carroll wrote this of his discipline: "Science isn't in the business of proving things. Rather, science judges the merits of competing models in terms of their simplicity, clarity, comprehensiveness, and fit to the data. Unsuccessful theories are never disproven, as we can always concoct elaborate schemes to save the phenomena; they just fade away as better theories gain acceptance."[4]

---

4. Sean Carroll, "Does the Universe Need God?," in *The Blackwell Companion to Science and Christianity*, ed. J. B. Stump and Alan G. Padgett (Oxford: Wiley-Blackwell, 2012), 196.

History, like science, is a public discipline. Like scientists, historians state their theories, publish the reasons they have for believing them, and then invite their peers to offer critique. Carroll mentions four criteria: simplicity, clarity, comprehensiveness, and fit to the data. Allow me to restate his criteria, add to them, and thereby show how historians critique their own beliefs as well as those of others.

— Simplicity: Is the theory simpler than its rivals (Ockham's razor)? Simply put (no pun intended), simpler theories are less likely to be flawed than are more complex theories.
— Clarity: Is the theory clearly stated? Unclear theories cannot be tested.
— Comprehensiveness: Does the theory account for all the available data? Coherency and simplicity are much more easily attained if one disregards some of the data, but then the conclusion is more likely to be flawed. Comprehensiveness serves as a guard to overemphasizing simplicity. Thus historians usually need to be satisfied with choosing a model that is more comprehensive than its competitors over one that is less comprehensive.
— Correlation (fit to data): Does the theory seem, as best we can tell, to describe how things actually are as we experience them? Truth is sometimes counterintuitive, but generally common sense is a reliable guide.
— Coherence: Does the theory fit with other theories that have strong support? If a theory requires that the historian jettison another theory that is widely accepted, that should give the historian pause. It could still be correct, but the probability of this being the case is not high. When two theories conflict, historians should reassess the evidence supporting each theory.
— Fruitfulness: Does the theory answer a lingering question to which there has previously been no satisfying answer?
— Predictability: Can one make predictions based on the theory? Experiments come from theories that make

predictions. Though this is of more use in the hard sciences than in history, it can still be applied to some degree in history by asking hypothetical questions, projecting what would probably be the result if the proposed model were correct, and then seeing if any historical evidence fits with the hypothetical result.

By now it should be obvious that historical reasoning involves a unique sort of logic, what is called *abductive reasoning*.[5] Abduction, a type of pragmatic reasoning, was given its formal name by Charles Sanders Peirce (1839–1914).[6] Peirce did not invent abduction; human beings have always practiced it. He did, however, give formal expression to something that people have always done, thus allowing future reasoning of this sort to be done in a more critically aware and consistent manner.

Abductive reasoning is neither deductive nor inductive. Abductive reasoning, even when done properly, doesn't lead to a *certain conclusion*, as deductive reasoning does; nor even necessarily to a *probable conclusion*, as inductive reasoning does; but rather to the *most plausible* conclusion, meaning the likeliest explanation for the observations. One must note that *sometimes the best abductive explanation is still incorrect:* sometimes truth is less plausible than fiction. Furthermore, *abductive conclusions depend on the available evidence*. Rarely do historians have access to all the evidence they would like to have. Therefore, historical conclusions must be revised when additional evidence becomes available, from which more effective explanations can come. Abduction also means that *sometimes historians encounter situations for which they have no present explanation*.

Abductive reasoning is pragmatic and subjective because plausibility is at least to some degree in the eye of the beholder. One should note, however, that abductive reasoning is not only

---

5. For accessible, brief treatments of abduction, see the essays in Umberto Eco, "Horns, Hooves, and Insteps: Some Hypotheses on Three Types of Abduction," in *The Sign of Three: Dupin, Holmes, Peirce*, ed. Umberto Eco and Thomas A. Sebeok (Bloomington: Indiana University Press, 1988).

6. See Charles S. Peirce, *Philosophical Writings of Peirce*, ed. Justus Buchler (New York: Dover Publications, 1955), esp. 150–56, 190–217; Peirce, *Collected Papers of Charles Sanders Peirce*, ed. Charles Hartshorne, Paul Weiss, and Arthur Banks (Cambridge, MA: Harvard University Press, 1935–1966), esp. vol. 5, book 1, lectures 6–7; Peirce, *Chance, Love, and Logic* (New York: Harcourt Brace, 1923).

subjective but also *critical*. As we have seen, historical reasoning is conducted by standards or broad rules on which there is general agreement.

The chart below shows other ways in which history is similar to the theoretical sciences.

Comparison	
History	Science
History is the human attempt to understand the past.	Science is the human attempt to understand nature.
History has well-developed principles for how to determine what is true.	Science has well-developed principles for how to determine what is true.
Any practitioner should adhere to these principles.	Any practitioner should adhere to these principles.
There is a large body of knowledge accepted by the experts.	There is a large body of knowledge accepted by the experts.
Some things are not agreed upon by the experts.	Some things are not agreed upon by the experts.
There are some well-accepted tenets that probably will not be discarded, though they may be refined.	There are some well-accepted tenets that probably will not be discarded, though they may be refined.
Our understanding may change with new data.	Our understanding may change with new data.
Our understanding may change with new theories of interpretation/inference, which may result in new conclusions.	Our understanding may change with new theories of interpretation/inference, which may result in new conclusions.

In addition, both historians and theoretical scientists make use of models in their work. In science, a model is not to be confused with the phenomenon it describes but is rather a useful shorthand that (hopefully) is true so far as it goes. For example, hydrogen may be modeled as its atomic number in the periodic table, or as Niels Bohr's model picturing a single electron orbiting a proton, or as Erwin Schrödinger's wave equation. *Yet none of these models actually is hydrogen!*[7] Still, there is much that we believe to be true about hydrogen in each of these models, based upon abductive testing of them. In a similar but unique way, historians model the historical figures they study. Schweitzer famously put forward the model of Jesus as an apocalyptic Jewish messiah, whereas Wrede pictured Jesus' messiahship as the theological creation of the early church. In research today there are many competing models for Jesus, such as cynic, sage, or political revolutionary, to name just a few. The upshot of all this is that *the historical Jesus will never be the real Jesus* any more than the atomic number 1 is really hydrogen or the historical Julius Caesar is the real Caesar. The historical Jesus is merely a sketch of the real Jesus constructed from the inferences that historians make, given the available evidence. This does not mean that statements about the historical Jesus are never true; they are true insofar as they match what Jesus really did and said.

The authors of the New Testament Gospels were acting as historians. They sought to convey to their readers the authentic message of Jesus. Therefore, it is appropriate for historians to critique the Gospels as they would assess any other ancient text, regardless of their theological position. Historians may believe that the Gospels are the Word of God, or texts through which a *Sitz im Leben* of an early Christian community is communicated, or the theology of an evangelist, or something else, but as historians they should treat the Gospels as historical documents. In the same way that inspired speech cannot get around the law of noncontradiction, so the Gospels cannot avoid historical criticism. Just as the Psalms are assessed with regard to

---

7. Thanks to Martinez Hewlett for this insight. Martinez Hewlett, "The Evolution Wars: Who Is Fighting with Whom about What?" in *Intelligent Design: William A. Demski and Michael Ruse in Dialogue*, ed. Robert B. Stewart (Minneapolis: Fortress Press, 2007), 46.

meter, so the Gospels must be subjected to the methodological questions that historians ask. The Gospels may be *more than historical documents* in that they clearly are meant to convey a theological message as well as a historical record, but they cannot be *less than historical documents*.

So, how exactly should the historian proceed? I propose that historians be as charitable as possible toward texts (and the authors who stand behind them) but at the same time as critical as possible in their evaluation of texts when it comes to assessing their historical reliability. We should give them the benefit of the doubt as to reliability—and then critique them as to how they fare when compared with the evidence. Charity and critique are not mutually exclusive.

How does one read the Gospels charitably yet also critically? I offer a model with four proposals:

Proposal 1. All New Testament historians, whether Christian or non-Christian, conservative or liberal, should be as skeptical about their skepticism as they are of other historians' conclusions. Skepticism is demanding evidence before believing; cynicism is not believing even with evidence. Therefore, they need to be aware of their own presuppositions and as a result be conscious of ways in which their presuppositions might lead them to overlook or distort the evidence. Presuppositions are not things that only others have! (Bultmann recognized this.)[8]

Proposal 2. History, like the sciences, is a public discipline, subject to critique and correction. For that reason responsible New Testament historians will be involved in academic societies that allow input from all perspectives. In this way, the scholarly community will police itself.

Proposal 3. All New Testament historians, whether Christian or not, conservative or liberal, should situate the Gospels in the first-century Middle Eastern *predominantly* oral world. In particular, historians should situate the Gospels in the Second Temple period of the Jewish world, thus expecting to find some

---

8. Rudolf Bultmann, "Is Exegesis with Presuppositions Possible?," in *Existence and Faith: Shorter Writings of Rudolf Bultmann*, ed. Schubert M. Ogden (London: Collins, 1961), 342–52.

signs of first-century Jewish influence in Jesus' sayings but also signs of uniqueness or reasons why Jesus would be rejected by Jewish leaders. Astute readers will notice that I am proposing something like what N. T. Wright calls the criterion of double similarity and double dissimilarity, or what Gerd Theissen and Annette Merz refer to as the criterion of historical plausibility.[9] When historians find such signs, they should recognize them as marks of authenticity. For charity's sake they should not require such marks of authenticity but rather notice them when they are present. Given the occasional nature of historical evidence, scholars should think of the criteria that Jesus scholars use as criteria *of* authenticity rather than as criteria *required for* authenticity. I am inclined to think that virtually all of the criteria have their uses but that any of them can be abused. The crucial issue is not one of finding the right criteria (there is no silver bullet!) but rather of using criteria rightly. There is no substitute for sound historical judgment.

A word of warning to my fellow conservatives seems appropriate here. Just as the presuppositions and methods of the form critics could only have arisen in a culture that was primarily a literary culture, thus a culture very much unlike that of Jesus or the earliest Christians, conservatives need to be aware that many of our own presuppositions, historically speaking, are equally foreign in that they arise from Anglo-American systematic theological systems that are almost entirely foreign to the time of Jesus and his biographers. In other words, the historical Jesus may not look as much like an evangelical Protestant theologian as an American evangelical might expect.

Proposal 4. Because history is a public discipline, all historians should seek to apply what C. Stephen Evans calls Type 2 methodological naturalism. This fourth proposal needs to be unpacked. *Not all methodological naturalism is the same.* Evans helpfully distinguishes between Type 1 methodological naturalism and Type 2 methodological naturalism.

---

9. N. T. Wright, *Jesus and the Victory of God*, vol. 2 of *Christian Origins and the Question of God* (Minneapolis: Fortress Press, 1996), 131–33; Gerd Theissen and Annette Merz, *The Historical Jesus: A Comprehensive Guide*, trans. John Bowden (Minneapolis: Fortress Press, 1996), 115–18.

For the Type 1 methodological naturalist, bracketing supernatural activity as a historical explanation is *obligatory*, thus holding that anyone who appeals to the supernatural as a historical explanation is not doing history correctly. A Type 1 methodological naturalist insists that historical explanations are *necessarily naturalistic*. A Type 2 methodological naturalist chooses to work without appealing to theological authorities, "without regarding that method as obligatory for historians."[10]

Historians must take every precaution to ensure that as far as possible their metaphysical presuppositions don't intrude on their historical investigation. Metaphysics operating *as an authority* is a frequent problem with historical work done concerning religious figures. Type 1 methodological naturalism is one example of this. Even when given sufficient evidence to conclude that the best explanation might be one in which the supernatural has played some role, Type 1 methodological naturalists refuse to consider supernatural explanations.

The opposite extreme is when a believer allows metaphysical beliefs to guide the historical investigation. Faced with sufficient evidence to conclude that the likeliest explanation is not supernatural, a believer may instead appeal to a less likely explanation for no obvious historical reason. Type 2 methodological naturalism does not allow either extreme.

I am proposing something similar to natural theology. Natural theology is the attempt to learn as much as possible about God's existence and attributes on the basis of reason and nature alone. As a philosopher, I frequently work as a natural theologian. As a systematic theologian, I engage in a type of revealed theology. As a natural theologian, I acknowledge my theistic presuppositions; because of them, supernatural explanations are a live option for me, but *I do not allow my faith to operate as a historical authority*. My metaphysical beliefs broaden the range of possible explanations that I consider, but they do not determine the explanation that I choose.

---

10. C. Stephen Evans, "Methodological Naturalism in Historical Biblical Scholarship," in *Jesus and the Restoration of Israel: A Critical Assessment of N. T. Wright's "Jesus and the Victory of God,"* ed. Carey C. Newman (Downers Grove: InterVarsity Press, 1999), 184.

How does this work in practice? A Type 1 methodological naturalist could conclude—*as a historian*—that the best explanation for the radical mutation of Jewish belief concerning resurrection that was characteristic of the earliest Christians (one man, Jesus, rather than all the righteous dead, was resurrected in the middle of history, rather than at the end of time) was that Jesus' followers *believed* that he was raised from the dead. But a Type 1 methodological naturalist could not—*as a historian*—conclude that Jesus being raised from the dead was the best explanation for their belief. A Type 2 methodological naturalist could go further and thus conclude—*as a historian*—that the best explanation for their belief that Jesus was raised from the dead was that Jesus actually had been raised from the dead.[11] A Type 2 methodological naturalist could conclude from a charitable yet critical evaluation of the evidence that this explanation had more explanatory power than any other explanation available at the time.

TRUSTING HISTORICAL TEXTS

The title of this book is *Can We Trust the Bible on the Historical Jesus?*[12] What does it mean, however, to *trust a text*? One question that immediately arises is this: "Must the Gospels be inerrant for them to be trusted as historical texts?" The short answer is no. This is a simple question to answer because of the part-whole relation that obtains between inerrancy and historical reliability. Historical reliability is a component of inerrancy. In other words, historical reliability is a *necessary condition* of inerrancy. Inerrancy, on the other hand, is a *sufficient condition* for historical reliability. If a text is inerrant, then it necessarily is historically reliable (if it relates to some historical state of affairs); but merely being historically reliable is not enough for one to know that a

---

11. N. T. Wright, *The Resurrection of the Son of God*, vol. 3 of *Christian Origins and the Question of God* (Minneapolis: Fortress Press, 2003), 372, 686.
12. That was the title of the conference in which the dialogue took place. The discussion focuses on the Gospels, yet with a few comments on Acts.

text is inerrant because that text may contain errors that are not historical in nature. For instance, the text could contain scientific errors, legal errors, theological errors, and so forth. Thus inerrancy requires historical reliability but not vice versa.

What is required for a text to be historically reliable? Before we can answer this question, we must understand what it would mean for a single statement[13] to be considered historically reliable. First, it must be a historical statement, meaning a statement that has a past state of affairs as its referent. "I'm thirsty" is a statement, but it is not a historical statement. Therefore only texts that are intended to inform readers about the past can be historically reliable. This means that questions of genre enter into the discussion. The four New Testament Gospels and Acts fall within the genre of history.[14] Second, it must accurately describe that state of affairs.[15] "Abraham Lincoln was the first president of the United States" is a historical statement but not a true statement.

But must each historical statement of a text be true for the text generally to be considered historically reliable? This then is the question that interests me: "Can a text still be considered historically reliable even if one or more of the historical statements in that text is possibly false?" Obviously, if such a text contains false statements, then it is not inerrant, but we've already established that inerrancy and historical reliability are not the same thing. In other words, may we reasonably judge a historical text to be reliable even if we judge it to be only *generally true* but not *comprehensively true* in everything that it affirms?[16] In asking about a hypothetical text that *we judge* to be only generally true, I am seeking to avoid the sort of question-begging that follows from believing in advance that a text (the New Testament?) is either true or false. Note well:

---

13. A "statement" is a sentence that has a truth value: it must either be true or false. Commands, questions, and proposals are not statements, yet they may be sentences.
14. Acts is not the same sort of historical book as the Gospels; Acts is theological history, while the Gospels are theological biographies, i.e., biographies written with a theological agenda.
15. I am obviously here appealing to a correspondence theory of truth.
16. This is purely a supposal on my part, i.e., I am not prejudging the issue in one way or the other, either as a matter of historical method or theology. I am simply asking and seeking to answer a hypothetical question of historical method.

I am trying to ask and answer a *methodological question* rather than a *theological question*.

There are two ways to try to answer this question. One is to state theoretically what needs to be the case for a text to be considered generally reliable. This is an a priori approach, which is consistent with *epistemic methodism*.[17] After stating our theoretical standard for general reliability, we can then seek to see if any text measures up to that standard. The other approach is to see if there are any cases in which, in practice, we seem to consider a text still to be generally reliable although we have reason to think it contains at least one false statement. This would be an a posteriori approach, which would be consistent with *epistemic particularism*. Which approach should we adopt? Let's consider two examples, one that uses an a priori methodist approach and the other that uses an a posteriori particularist approach. In an effort to alleviate any concerns about prejudgments, I'm going to discuss persons being generally reliable rather than historical texts, and then hopefully we can draw some conclusions that will apply to texts.

Consider Ted Bundy and Ozzie Smith. Ted Bundy was a notorious serial killer and confessed to murdering thirty people. At what point, however, did Bundy become a murderer? An a priori methodist approach seems appropriate here. Our method can be spelled out thus:

1. The wrongful and intentional taking of a human life is murder.
2. Therefore, anyone who wrongfully and intentionally takes a human life is a murderer.

When Bundy wrongfully and intentionally killed that first person, he became a murderer. That seems obviously true, or at least it is noncontroversial.

---

17. René Descartes's "Cogito, ergo sum" (I think, therefore I am) is a classic example of epistemic methodism. Descartes states in advance what it would take to be certain that he is not being deceived (an indubitable belief) and then proceeds to doubt (Descartes's skepticism was not genuine but rather merely methodological) until he arrives at the belief that he was doubting, which he cannot doubt. René Descartes, *Discourse on Method*, Part IV.

Ozzie Smith is one of the greatest defensive players in baseball history. He was a Gold Glove shortstop thirteen times in his major-league career. At what point did Smith become an exceptional defensive player? An a priori methodist approach does not seem right here. Why? Because stating a method to know whether one is an outstanding defensive shortstop appears to be an impossible task. One might think that it is a simple matter of stating what would be an outstanding fielding percentage, but our method cannot be based simply on fielding percentage because that only measures how many errors a player has committed against how many chances the player had, how many balls were within reach. It does not measure how much ground a player can cover, how strong and accurate his arm is, or how quickly he can transition from catching the ball to throwing the ball. Therefore an a posteriori particularist approach seems appropriate here. Baseball historians know that Smith was one of the greatest defensive players in baseball history because they observed him and others play the position. For that reason they measure today's players against the standard that Smith set. Some statistics are relevant for our discussion, however. Smith's career fielding percentage was .9782,[18] which is an extraordinarily high percentage for a shortstop. That means that Smith fielded his position correctly almost 98 percent of the time. Still, over twenty shortstops have higher career fielding percentages. Smith also committed nearly 300 errors. Nevertheless, no baseball historian thinks that there have been twenty shortstops who fielded their position more efficiently than Smith did. Ozzie Smith was generally reliable and an all-time great, rightfully in the Hall of Fame.

Note that one example concerns matters of a disjunctive sort, matters in which one either is or is not. The other example concerns matters of degree and context, matters in which one is more or less something. Being a murderer is disjunctive, like being pregnant or being alive: you either are or you're not. Being an outstanding defensive shortstop is a question of degree and

---

18. "Baseball Reference," baseball-reference.com/leaders/fielding_perc_ss_career.shtml.

context, more like being overweight: a 300-pound sumo wrestler is not overweight, but a 300-pound jockey is. The question is thus posed: Historical reliability is more akin to which example? Being a murderer or being a Gold Glove infielder?

Does overall experience with a person tell us anything about whether we consider them reliable? Absolutely. All of us are sincerely mistaken from time to time. We all believe certain things, but some of our beliefs are false. We all know that everyone has false beliefs at one time or another, and yet we deem some people (generally) reliable.

For instance, I tell my son that the book I borrowed from him is on the dining room table because that's where I left it. Unbeknownst to me, after I left the house, my wife put the book on the bookshelf because that's where books belong. When my son cannot find the book, my wife explains to my understandably frustrated son what has happened. As a result he still regards me as someone he can trust because he knows that I did not intend to deceive him and that I accurately relayed the facts to him as I knew them to be. Nevertheless, what I told him was not true. Yet he still trusts me and considers me to be reliable.[19] He is operating as a particularist.

In a particularist approach, one would also examine how New Testament historians treat ancient historians and their texts. Consider Josephus: I don't know any New Testament historian who thinks that the works of Josephus are inerrant, thus comprehensively reliable. Nor do I know any New Testament historian who thinks that Josephus is unbiased (he was a politician). But I also don't know any New Testament historian who doesn't rely on the works of Josephus in some way to recreate the world in which Jesus and Paul lived as well as to confirm and augment what the New Testament Gospels tell us about certain historical figures. In other words, historians seem to believe that the works of Josephus are generally reliable.

---

19. This is actually how some scholars conceive of historical reliability, and even of inerrancy. In at least one work, E. J. Carnell allowed that inspiration guarantees only that the Scripture writers have accurately reproduced their sources; inerrancy did not guarantee that they would correct them. Edward J. Carnell, *The Case for Orthodox Theology* (Philadelphia: Westminster Press, 1959), 109–11. For a brief but substantial discussion of various ways of understanding inerrancy, see Millard J. Erickson, *Christian Theology*, 2nd ed. (Grand Rapids: Baker Book House, 1998), 246–65.

Josephus clearly had an agenda, but that doesn't disqualify his works. His writings do, however, need to be read critically. *But this is what historians should do with any text: critically assess it.* In the same way, the New Testament Gospels, when read critically, can be believed, even if one thinks that they are not entirely correct in everything they assert. They can serve as reliable guides even if their authors clearly have an agenda—which they admit that they do. Bart Ehrman, responding to mythicists (those who think Jesus never existed), says as much:

> I should stress that I am not saying that Luke and the other Gospel writers were trying to present disinterested accounts of the life of Jesus. These authors were anything but disinterested, and their biases need to be front and center in the critics' minds when evaluating what they have to say. . . . The fact that their books later became documents of faith has no bearing on the question of whether the books can still be used for historical purposes. To dismiss the Gospels from the historical record is neither fair nor scholarly.[20]

We also trust people whom we don't know that well but who have certain qualifications signifying that they should know what they're talking about. We go to doctors and take the drugs that they prescribe, yet without knowing them personally. We don't do this because we are easily taken in, but rather because we know that they've had years of medical training, and also because we know that they would stand to lose their livelihood if we were to die as a result of what they have prescribed. We have good reasons for thinking that they know what they are doing when it comes to medical treatment. Yet we also know that doctors can and do make mistakes. So on major medical decisions, it's wise to get a second opinion from an equally qualified physician working in the same field.

Still, writing history is obviously different from practicing medicine. But the relevant question is the same: is the person qualified to do a certain thing, whether it's prescribing medicine or relating historical events? A crucially important question

---

20. Bart D. Ehrman, *Did Jesus Exist? The Historical Argument for Jesus of Nazareth* (San Francisco: HarperOne, 2012), 73.

concerning the historical reliability of a historical text is this: "Was the author in position to know what was written?" So, were the authors of the Gospels in positions to know what they were writing about? The early church believed that Matthew and John were written by two of Jesus' original disciples, and that Mark and Luke were written by close associates of Peter and Paul, respectively. In fact, the early church *unanimously* attributed these books to Matthew, Mark, Luke, and John; their names appear in all extant manuscripts with titles. Still, the earliest Gospel manuscripts with their names come from the second century, so the early church could be mistaken on this point. Many believe that the early church was mistaken. Yet notice this: *historical reliability neither stands nor falls on this point*, although the case for historical reliability would be strengthened if the early church were correct on this point. Regardless of who authored them, the Gospels were almost certainly written in the first century, much closer to the events that they describe than almost any other ancient work. All other things being equal, the closer the historian is to the events related in a historical text, the greater the probability that they accurately relate the events about which they speak.[21] It seems, then, at least possible that the Gospels could be reliable sources concerning Jesus.

In large part, this is an issue of who has the burden of proof. Should we read the New Testament Gospels with an attitude of skepticism such that they are guilty until proved innocent? Or should we read them optimistically, yet also check all the relevant evidence?

WHAT'S AT STAKE?

What's at stake in asking whether we can trust what the Gospels say about Jesus as a historical figure? One thing that is not

---

21. There are, of course, some exceptions to this general rule. Sometimes a correct historical judgment requires historical distance. For instance, Neville Chamberlain (Prime Minister of the United Kingdom) believed that he had headed off hostilities in Europe when he negotiated the annexing of the Sudetenland to Germany in 1938. Some historical distance helps people see how wrong Chamberlain was.

at stake is Christianity. Believers were proclaiming the good news before the first Gospel was written. To think that God's actions in history depend upon reports of them is to confuse ontology with epistemology.

Nevertheless, this is a matter of existential significance. Depending on how readers interpret this dialogue, one's confidence in the historical reliability of Scripture could be significantly increased or diminished. Epistemic doubt can lead to existential anxiety. Or readers could be more confident that the New Testament Gospels can actually stand up to scrutiny, could even better understand the historical message in the Gospels, and could become better Bible readers themselves.

History is difficult, but history matters. History requires ongoing critique and never tells us everything we might want to know, which can be frustrating. Many have concluded, therefore, that the historical Jesus is unnecessary, that only the existential Christ of faith is needed. But the existential stakes of jettisoning history are enormous! The same apostle who declares that salvation comes from *believing in your heart* that God raised Jesus from the dead (Rom. 10:9) also insists that "if Christ has not been raised, your faith is futile and you are still in your sins" (1 Cor. 15:17). Paul believed that knowing historical truth about what Jesus said and did, and particularly whether or not he was raised from the dead, was crucially important.[22] So regardless of the difficulty of the task, the work must be done.

Debates are based on both disagreement and agreement. There must be some reciprocity on an issue; otherwise the opponents would talk past each other entirely. The debate that is recorded (hopefully in a historically reliable manner) in this book features two major New Testament scholars arguing for their own positions on a question that they both agree matters: "Can we trust the Bible on the historical Jesus?" Readers will note other points of agreement between Ehrman and Evans as well as numerous points of disagreement. Truth is not

---

22. The issue at hand in 1 Cor. 15 is not the resurrection of Jesus but rather the general resurrection of the righteous dead at the end of the age. Nevertheless, the conditionals in verses 17–19 do concern the resurrection of Jesus.

determined by scoring a debate, but hearing from those with whom one disagrees often sharpens one's thinking on an issue.

I have known Bart Ehrman and Craig Evans for more than a decade; I respect them as scholars and consider both to be friends. I also disagree with each of them at points. Nevertheless, I am a better person and a better scholar for my interaction with them. I trust that you too will benefit from reading this book.

Can We Trust the Bible on the Historical Jesus?

A Dialogue between Bart D. Ehrman and Craig A. Evans

[The title of the 2011 Greer-Heard Point-Counterpoint Forum and now the title of this book is Can We Trust the Bible on the Historical Jesus? *The focus is especially on the Gospels of the New Testament, with a few comments on Acts. In the body of the dialogue, the word "debate" sometimes refers to the dialogue. The conversation had opening statements and responses, but in other ways it was not quite a formal debate. Hence, we have chosen to use the term "dialogue" in the chapter subtitle. But for practical purposes, the two words are interchangeable. The dialogue that follows was intended for oral presentation—to be spoken and heard. As a courtesy to readers of this text, some small editorial changes to grammar have been made to facilitate smoother reading. Notes in the main body of Evans's discourse were written by Craig Evans and were part of his original paper from which he read during the oral presentation of his opening statement.]*

BART EHRMAN: OPENING STATEMENT

Well, thank you very much. It's a pleasure being with you today. The resolution that we are debating is "Can we trust the Bible on the historical Jesus?" Let me ask, how many of you think that we can trust the Bible on the historical Jesus? Right! How many are fairly sure that you are not going to agree with anything that I have to say? Well, it's a pleasure being with you anyway. Thank you, Bob, for this invitation, and thanks to the seminary for bringing me in. It is an honor to be with people with whom I disagree, and I appreciate very much the chance to tell you what I think and what I believe. I was here three years ago, having a discussion with Dan Wallace, and I enjoyed it very much and greatly appreciated being well received by a large group of people who completely disagreed with my views. And I certainly am looking forward to sharing my view with an equally worthy opponent, Craig Evans.

Let me begin by saying something about what I understand this resolution to mean. The question is posed: "Can we trust the Bible on the historical Jesus?" I take the term "we" to mean the people today, us. Not people in antiquity. Not people in the Middle Ages. Can we modern people—with modern sensibilities and modern understandings of the world, of history, and of research—trust what the Bible has to say about the historical Jesus? The *historical* Jesus. We will not be debating whether the Bible tells us great stories about Jesus, nor whether the Bible provides the basis for an adequate theology of Jesus. We are not debating the literary merits or the theological adequacy of the Bible. We are debating its historical reliability, and we are not asking whether the Bible writers did a good job by the standards of their day. We are talking about *our* day. Can we today trust that the Bible is historically reliable in what it has to say about Jesus? At the outset of this discussion, I should admit that when I began my study of the Bible, I very much believed that the answer was yes. I was a Bible-believing Christian attending the Moody Bible Institute of Chicago. At that time I held to the view of the Moody Bible Institute, which affirmed the verbal-plenary inspiration of Scripture. We believed that the Bible was inspired even to its very words, thus that it was completely inspired. This is similar, I think, to the Baptist Faith and Message 2000, which I quote: "The Holy Bible . . . has God for its author, salvation for its end, and truth, without any mixture of error, for its matter. Therefore, all Scripture is totally true and trustworthy."[1] But is that right? Is the Bible totally true? Without any mixture of error? That is the question that I will be addressing with you tonight.

As I said, I believed that when I was a student in the Moody Bible Institute. The more research I did on the matter, the more

---

1. Baptist Faith and Message 2000, http://www.sbc.net/bfm2000/bfm2000.asp.

I began to doubt it. Today I think I can say without reservation that, in fact, the Bible does contain errors and the Bible does contain mistakes with respect to the historical Jesus. And I will try to demonstrate that to you in my short time with you.

After I went to Moody Bible Institute, I went off to Wheaton College to finish my degree, which is in English literature. I learned Greek at Wheaton College and became interested in studying the Greek New Testament. The expert in Greek manuscripts of the New Testament was a scholar named Bruce M. Metzger, who happened to teach at Princeton Theological Seminary. I decided that I wanted to study with the world expert, so I went to that seminary. While I was at Princeton, I learned many things. Princeton, of course, is a Presbyterian school, training Presbyterian ministers. As a ministerial school, it is very theological, although the professors at Princeton Theological Seminary did not hold to the inerrancy of the Bible. They did have a very high view of Scripture, but they allowed that, in fact, there could be some mistakes. At Princeton Theological Seminary I learned a different way of reading the Bible, a manner different from the way most people today read the Bible. Now, I don't know about people in New Orleans, but I do know about people in Chapel Hill, and I can say how most people there seem to read the Bible. First of all, most people don't read the Bible at all in my experience. I teach a very large class of undergraduate students at Chapel Hill, and as a rule they have a far greater commitment to the Bible than knowledge about the Bible. They are really sure the Bible is true, but they have never bothered to read it. Students who do read the Bible tend to do it in one of two ways. One way is what I call the "Ouija-board approach." That's when you have a question for God and open up the Bible [at random] to find the answer. There it is, in that verse. That is what I call the Ouija-board approach, which many people use. The other way people read the Bible—as people typically read if they are seriously reading the Bible—is what I call reading "vertically": they start at the top of the page and read to the bottom of the page. And you ask, What's wrong with that? Well, there is nothing wrong with that. Of course, that's how you should read the Bible. You should read every book like that. You start at the top, you go to the bottom, then you go to the next page: top to bottom. You start at the beginning of the book and go to the end of the book.

Now when you read the Bible like that, especially the New Testament Gospels, it has a certain effect on you. You start at the beginning with the Gospel of Matthew, Matthew chapter 1, verse 1. And you read through Matthew from top to bottom, vertically. When you read Matthew vertically, you find out a lot about Jesus: Jesus' birth, Jesus' ministry, Jesus' miracles, his teaching, his death, and his resurrection. And then you go to the Gospel of Mark, and you find, in fact, that it's a very similar story: Jesus' life, his miracles, his teachings, his death, his resurrection. It sounds a lot like Matthew. And then you read Luke, and it sounds a lot like Matthew and Mark: the birth of Jesus, the life of Jesus, the miracles, the teachings, the death and resurrection. You get to the Gospel of John, and it seems different, but it's all basically the same thing. It's the life of Jesus, his miracles, his teachings, his death and resurrection. It all sounds the same because of the way you are reading it, vertically, from beginning to end. The Gospels sound very similar to one another.

Another way to read the Bible, though, is to read it horizontally rather than vertically. A horizontal reading of the Bible is not to be done to the exclusion of the vertical reading; it's simply a different way to read the Bible, especially the Gospels. The way it works is this: you read a story in one of the Gospels, and then you read the same story in another Gospel. Then you compare the stories. It's as if you have the Gospels lined up in columns next to each other, and you read across the columns, perusing them horizontally instead of vertically. When you do so, you compare the Gospels carefully with one another.

When you read the Bible in that way, when you read it horizontally, you begin to find mistakes as you compare what one Gospel says about Jesus with what another Gospel says about Jesus in the same story. Let me give you a couple of examples. I should say at the beginning that I was not looking for mistakes when I started reading the Bible this way. I did not want to find mistakes when I started reading the Bible this way. I was reluctant to find mistakes when I read the Bible this way. But I started finding mistakes when I read the Bible this way. As a good conservative Christian, I was not someone who was particularly put off by the big differences in the Bible because I could reconcile those fairly easily. So when the Gospel of Matthew says that the followers of Jesus need to keep the law and Paul says the followers of Jesus do not have to keep the law, I did not have trouble reconciling those two things. When Mark's Jesus is portrayed as very human, and John's Jesus is portrayed as very divine, I did not have trouble reconciling those two things. When I started out, I had trouble reconciling the *little things*, the tiny things.

For example, in Mark 5:21–43 is the famous story of Jesus healing Jairus's daughter. The way the story goes is that Jesus is beside the sea, and a ruler of the synagogue, Jairus by name, comes up to him; on seeing Jesus, he falls down before his feet and beseeches him many times, saying, "My daughter is ill; come and lay your hands on her so that you can save her, and she will live." Jesus goes off to Jairus's house, but before he gets very far, a woman comes up from behind—this woman who has had a hemorrhage for twelve years—and touches Jesus' robe because she wants to be healed of her sickness. Jesus turns and asks, "Who has touched me?," because he has realized that power has gone out from him. The woman ends up getting healed, but because of this incident, Jesus is delayed from going to Jairus's house. While he is delayed, some servants come from Jairus's house, and they come to Jairus and say, "It's too late. Your daughter has died." Jesus tells them not to worry, he goes to the house, and he raises her from the dead. Beautiful story in Mark, chapter 5.

The Gospel of Matthew has the same story. And when you read the Gospels horizontally, you find something very interesting. What happens in Matthew's Gospel [9:18–26] is that this leader in the synagogue comes up, worships Jesus, and says to him, "My daughter has just now died. Come and lay your hands on her so that she will live."

But wait a second: in Mark's Gospel she was sick but hadn't died yet, and because Jesus was delayed, she died in the interim. But in Matthew's Gospel she is dead before Jairus even comes to Jesus. Well, which is it? You might say, "Who really cares? The girl died, and Jesus raised her from the dead." Yes, that's enough if you are just interested in a good story; they are both really good stories. But this is the kind of detail that started making me think, "Why is it that the stories are different?" They can't both be right: the girl was either dead before Jairus came to Jesus, or she died while Jairus was talking to Jesus. It can't be both in the same happening. Somebody has changed the story. If they changed the story in little ways, how do you know they didn't change it in big ways? You don't have to take my word for it that somebody changed the story; read the story horizontally yourself.

Now, I have students who find this kind of little detail really insignificant, even immaterial: "Who really cares?" So, I tell my students that it is like what happens when a detective shows up on the crime scene. Somebody has been murdered and is lying in a pool of blood. The detective comes into the room, and what does he start doing? He starts looking for fingerprints or a strand of hair. And you say, "Why are you looking for fingerprints and a strand of hair? There is a *dead body* here!" Yes, but to solve the crime you have to find the evidence, and sometimes the evidence is the smallest little thing. When I was an evangelical Christian, convinced that the Bible had no errors of any kind, I had to deal with the problem that there were differences among the Gospels that could not be reconciled with one another. Some of these differences were small, little, but they were differences. And how do you reconcile those?

The Last Supper. Before Jesus' death he is having his Last Supper with his disciples, and he tells Peter, according to the Gospel of Matthew [26:34], "Before the cock crows you will deny me three times." When you read the same story in the Gospel of Mark [14:30], Jesus tells Peter, "Before the cock crows twice you will deny me three times." Well, which is it? Is it before the cock crows or before the cock crows twice?

In stereo. When I was at Moody Bible Institute, I bought a book that explained little differences like this. This is a book by a guy who wanted to show that even though we do have differences among the Gospels, they can all be reconciled. The book was called *The Life of Christ in Stereo.*[2] The idea is that you get four speakers, you see, and you get surround sound. The author took the four Gospels and spliced them all together, creating a surround sound of the Gospels where there are no differences. And he dealt with this problem that in Matthew the cock has to crow and in Mark it has to crow twice. His solution was that Peter denies Jesus *six* times: three times before the cock crows, and three times before the cock crows twice. Well, that's an interesting solution. But to create the solution, the author of the book actually wrote his own gospel, different from the four Gospels of the New Testament. I should point out, by the way, that when Peter denies Jesus in the fulfillment of the prophecy, he denies him to different people in the different Gospels. What's that all about? It's about somebody changing the story.

There are changes in all sorts of stories throughout the New Testament. You can start at the very beginning of the New Testament: the genealogies of Jesus. My students wonder why we have genealogies of Jesus at all. The interesting thing about these genealogies—there is one in Matthew, chapter 1, and there is one in Luke, chapter 3—is that both are genealogies of Joseph. So Joseph's father is so-and-so, and his grandfather is so-and-so, and his great-grandfather is so-and-so: they are genealogies of Joseph. And my students ask, "Why do you have a genealogy of Joseph?" They wonder about this because in both Matthew and Luke, Jesus is born of a virgin. In other words, Joseph is not the biological father. So why do these Gospels trace the bloodline of the father if Jesus is not related to the bloodline? That's a good question. I guess we need to assume that Joseph adopted Jesus or something like that. But what's interesting is that when you compare the genealogies, they in fact are different

---

2. J. M. Cheney, *The Life of Christ in Stereo: The Four Gospels Combined as One* (Portland, OR: Western Baptist Seminary Press [1969]).

genealogies. Who was Joseph's father? Was it James as in Matthew or Eli as in Luke? Who was his grandfather? Was it Matthan as in Matthew or was it Matthat as in Luke? Who was his great-grandfather? Eleazar or Levi? His great-great-grandfather, Eliud or Melchi? These are different genealogies, yet they are both said to be genealogies of Joseph. How can they both be right? Did Joseph have two fathers and two grandfathers and two great-grandfathers [in the line traced through David]?

With the birth of Jesus in the Gospel of Luke, we have a quite interesting account of how it is that Jesus came to be born in Bethlehem. Now in this case we are not dealing with a discrepancy: we are dealing with something that I think you would probably want to call a historical implausibility. I think many haven't thought about this particular passage in the Gospel of Luke. So, the way it works is this. Joseph and Mary are from the town of Nazareth. And we are told in Luke 2:1 that there was a census—when Caesar Augustus was the emperor—when all the world had to be taxed. Everybody had to register for this tax. Well, Joseph's lineage comes from the town of Bethlehem because he is in the line of King David, and David was born in Bethlehem. And so Joseph has to go from Nazareth to Bethlehem to register for this tax. Mary is fully pregnant at this time. He takes her with him and, as it turns out, when they are in Bethlehem, Mary gives birth. And then we are told that after she gives birth, eight days later Jesus is circumcised, according to the law. And we are told that after they fulfill the rites of Mary's purification, they return home to Nazareth. The rites of purification refer to Leviticus, chapter 12. When a woman gives birth, she is ceremonially impure. It doesn't mean she sinned or anything. She is ceremonially impure, and she has to perform a sacrifice to get rid of the ceremonial impurity. That happens thirty-three days after her son's circumcision. And so that's what they do. Jesus is circumcised on his eighth day, and thirty-three days later Mary is purified. So forty or forty-one days after Jesus' birth, they return to Nazareth.

Two things about this: First of all, many people have not thought much about this census. What does one make of this kind of census? This is a census when Caesar Augustus was the emperor, and everybody in the world had to register for it, we are told. Now, I assume that it doesn't mean China, but it probably means the entire Roman Empire. Joseph goes to Bethlehem because he is descended from David. But David lived a thousand years before Joseph. So, you mean everybody in the Roman Empire is returning to their ancestral home from a thousand years earlier?

Let's suppose that the U.S. Senate changes course and decides that we are going to have to pay more taxes. They are going to raise our taxes, but it will entail a special tax. This new tax will involve all of us registering for it, so there is going to be a census. And we all have to return to the homes of our ancestors from a thousand years ago. Where are you going to go? And can you imagine the entire Roman Empire doing this? What is odd is that it's not mentioned in any other ancient historical source. It didn't get in the newspapers? This is completely implausible. Why does Luke say it then? Because Luke knows full well that Jesus has to be born in Bethlehem, but he came from Nazareth. Well, if he came from Nazareth how did he get born in Bethlehem? Well, you see there was this census, and everybody had to go and register. So he tells a story.

Not only is the story implausible, but the story also seems to contradict the Gospel of Matthew. Matthew doesn't say anything about a census; Matthew indicates that Jesus was born in Bethlehem, and there is no word about his parents having come from anywhere else: they appear to be from Bethlehem. After Jesus is born, according to Matthew, the wise men come, following a star. They follow the star to Bethlehem, and the star stops over the house that Jesus is in. That's a very interesting phenomenon itself, when you think about it. Go outside on some starry night and ask yourself, "Which house is this star over?" This must be a special star. The directors of movies in Hollywood have to figure out how to make a star stand over a house. And the best movie that does this is the silent *Ben-Hur*. You all probably know the *Ben-Hur* with Charlton Heston from the 1950s. There is a silent *Ben-Hur* made in the 1920s, and what happened in that account is that the star leads the wise men to Bethlehem, and then it stops, and then a ray comes down to the house. That's how you know which house he's in.

In Matthew, the star leads the wise men to Jesus, they worship Jesus, and they offer three gifts. They are warned in a dream to go back some other way and not to tell King Herod where Jesus has been born because Herod is out to kill the child. Herod sends out the troops to kill every male two years and under in Bethlehem. This is according to the Gospel of Matthew. Joseph and Mary learn that Herod is out to kill the child, and so Joseph takes his family and flees to Egypt. And when they learn in Egypt that Herod is no longer the king but his son Archelaus is, they return; but they can't return to Judea because Archelaus is worse than his father, Herod. And so they relocate to Nazareth. Jesus then is raised in Nazareth. And so, in Matthew he is born in Bethlehem but in a story line different from Luke. Moreover, ask yourself this. If Matthew is right that they fled Bethlehem and went to Egypt and stayed there until Herod died, how can Luke be right that some forty days after Jesus' birth they returned to Nazareth? Somebody is not only changing stories but also making up stories; after all, you can't have it both ways.

These accounts of Jesus' birth are matched by accounts of Jesus' death. When did Jesus die? It's a very simple question. It's a historical question. Both Mark and John indicate that Jesus dies sometime during the Passover Feast, when Jews eat the Passover meal. Mark is quite explicit that Jesus dies the morning *after* the Passover meal is eaten; John is equally explicit on that timing. But in John 19:14, Jesus is crucified not in the morning but in the afternoon on the day *before* the Passover is eaten. How can it be both ways? Somebody has changed the story.

How did Judas die? Matthew says he hanged himself. The book of Acts says that he fell forward and his bowels poured out on the earth. When Judas died, who bought the field called the Field of Blood? Did Judas buy it with the money he got, or did the high priest buy it when Judas returned the money to the priests after Judas betrayed Jesus? It depends on whether you trust Matthew or Acts. Why is it called the Field of Blood? Is it because it was purchased with blood money or because Judas bled all over the field? It depends on which account you read.

Sometimes the differences among the compared Gospels and Acts really matter.

Then there are the resurrection narratives; do a horizontal reading of Matthew, Mark, Luke, and John on the resurrection for yourself. What happened at the resurrection? It depends on which account you read. Who went to the tomb? Was it Mary Magdalene by herself, or was it Mary Magdalene with other women? If with other women, which other women? It depends on which Gospel you read. What were the women named? It depends on which Gospel you read. Was the stone in front of the tomb, or was it already rolled away? It depends on which Gospel you read. What did they see there? Did they see a man there? Did they see two men there? Or did they see an angel there? It depends on which Gospel you read. Are the women told to tell the disciples to meet Jesus in Galilee, or are they told to tell the disciples that Jesus will appear to them, as he *said*, in Galilee? It depends on which Gospel you read. Do the women tell anybody? Mark says no; Matthew says yes. Are the disciples supposed to go to Galilee, or are they supposed to stay in Jerusalem? Matthew says that they are supposed to go to Galilee and that they do go to Galilee. Luke says that they are supposed to stay in Jerusalem and that they do stay in Jerusalem. In Luke, it's quite explicit that they don't leave Jerusalem; they stay there until the Day of Pentecost. But not according to Matthew: in Matthew they go to Galilee right away.

You say, "Well, that's the kind of thing you would expect, given the greatest miracle the world has ever seen. People would be excited and so moved that they wouldn't be able to get their story straight." Fair enough. But remember what we are debating. Are the accounts historically reliable or not? If everyone has changed the story and no one can get the story straight, let alone right, they might be terrific literary works and valuable theological works, but they are not historically accurate. Maybe historical accuracy doesn't matter. In that case, the debated resolution should not be whether we can trust what the Bible says historically but whether it matters what the Bible says historically.

Sometimes the differences are not discrepancies but difference in emphases. I will give you an example. What was Jesus' demeanor going to his death? In Mark's Gospel—the shortest Gospel, in many ways the most graphic—Jesus is betrayed. He is put on trial before Pontius Pilate, and he says only two words at his trial. Otherwise he is completely silent. In Mark's Gospel he is led off to be crucified after being betrayed and denied; his disciples have all fled, and Jesus is silent the entire way. You get the sense in Mark that Jesus is in shock. They nail him to the cross, and Jesus is silent in Mark's Gospel. Both of the others being crucified with Jesus mock him. People passing by mock him, the soldiers mock him, the dying robbers mock him. And at the end Jesus cries out, the only words he says in the entire proceeding, "My God, my God, why have you forsaken me?" And he dies. That's Mark's version.

Luke's version is quite different. In Luke's version, Jesus is not silent on the way to be crucified. In Luke's version, Jesus is going to be crucified, Simon is carrying the cross, and Jesus looks at the side of the road and sees women weeping for him. And he turns his head to them and says, "Daughters of Jerusalem, don't weep for me. Weep for yourselves and for your children for the fate that is to befall you." In Luke's Gospel, Jesus is not in shock. He doesn't wonder why God has forsaken him. He knows what's happening to him, and he is more concerned about these people by the side of the road than he is about himself. While being nailed to the cross, in Luke's Gospel he is not silent. Instead, Jesus prays, "Father, forgive them, for they don't know what they are doing." In Luke's Gospel, Jesus actually has an intelligent conversation with one of the two others being crucified with him. In Luke's Gospel, one of these mocks Jesus, and the other person tells him to be quiet because Jesus has done nothing to deserve this fate. And he turns his head to Jesus and says, "Lord, remember me when you come into your kingdom." This is only in Luke. Jesus turns his head to him, "Truly I tell you, today you will be with me in paradise." In Luke's Gospel, Jesus is not in shock; he knows exactly what's happening to him, he knows why it's happening to him, and he knows what's going to happen to him after it happens to him. He is going to wake up in paradise, and this guy is going to be with him.

Most telling of all, in Luke's Gospel Jesus does not cry out, "My God, my God, why have you forsaken me?" Instead, in Luke's Gospel Jesus prays, "Father, into your hands I commit my spirit," and then he dies. Luke's Gospel portrays Jesus as calm and in control until the very end, assured of God's presence with him. That's not the portrayal of Mark.

What people have done is that they have taken Mark and they have taken Luke and they have smashed them together into one big gospel, so that Jesus says and does everything in both accounts. Then they throw in Matthew for good measure, and they throw in John for good measure, and you end up with the seven last sayings of the dying Jesus; this whole group of seven sayings are found in precisely none of the Gospels.

If you do that, you need to realize that in effect you have written your own gospel. In order to reconcile the canonical Gospels, you have written your own account, which is not like any of the four. Now you are free to do that—it's a free country—but realize that, when you do so, you are saying that you should not pay attention precisely to what Mark has to say, you should not pay attention to what Luke has to say, you should pay attention to what *you* have to say; your gospel, rather than Matthew, Mark, Luke, or John. You have robbed each author of his own authorial integrity by making him say something that he doesn't say.

Some of the differences about Jesus among the various Gospels are quite significant and affect how we understand the historical Jesus. My view is that you need to read each Gospel for what it has to say because there are discrepancies and differences among them. You can't simply trust these accounts to give you historically accurate versions of what happened in the life of Jesus because they are not interested in providing historically accurate accounts of what happened in the life of Jesus.

These are Gospels; they are proclaiming good news. They are not histories. They are not objective biographies. They are filled with historical mistakes. But the authors were not trying to write objective historical accounts. They were trying to proclaim the good news.

Can we trust the Bible on the historical Jesus? Suppose over the next thirty years we ask four people to write biographies of Jimmy Carter. These four people, until now, have never heard of Jimmy Carter. They are not allowed to go to the library and do any research. They are not allowed to look at other historically written documents. They can rely only on oral reports, on what they have heard about Jimmy Carter. But they also are allowed to use one another's works. These four biographies are then gathered together and examined. They are all quite moving and powerful, but in a great number of places they contradict each other—often in small ways and indeed often in large ways. In a number of places these four accounts contradict what historians know about the facts of history. And in yet other places they make claims for what Carter did that are clearly impossible.

Would you say that these accounts could be trusted to give you a historically reliable narrative? Or would you say that if you want these sources to be true to history, you need to figure out where there are errors, mistakes, alterations of historical facts, contradictions, exaggerations, and biased reporting? If the latter, then you are saying that you cannot trust them as historical sources. The Bible also cannot be trusted as a historical source. It may provide great literature, and you may choose to use it for your theological beliefs, but it is not historically accurate. Thank you very much.

CRAIG EVANS: OPENING STATEMENT

Can we trust what the New Testament says about the historical Jesus? In a word, yes. If I did not trust what the New Testament says about Jesus, then it would not be easy to be a Christian.

Perhaps it would not be possible, at least not in any traditional or orthodox sense. But the question that I have raised requires some qualification. I have asked about the "historical Jesus," not Christology. I assume that focus on the historical Jesus excludes most of what is said about Jesus outside the Gospels themselves, where he is described as the risen, glorified, returning Son of God. I assume that speaking of the historical Jesus sets aside a variety of theological affirmations, such as the atoning and saving value of Jesus' death. After all, a historian can argue persuasively that Jesus indeed died on a Roman cross, but how can a historian, on the basis of the kind of evidence that historians examine, argue one way or another as to the value of Jesus' death in the sight of God? Accordingly, I limit my remarks to the four New Testament Gospels.

I shall speak to four questions. The *first* question is general and asks about the nature of the evidence. How much do we have, and how good is it? Here it will be helpful to compare the evidence for Jesus with the evidence for other figures of history and to compare how well preserved the New Testament Gospels are with other historical writings of late antiquity. The *second* question is narrower and asks about the practices of writing and publishing in late antiquity, such as how manuscripts were copied, gathered, studied, compared, corrected, and the like. Here I shall inquire into what we have learned from the thousands of papyri that have been unearthed, mostly in Egypt, in the last century and a half. The *third* question inquires into the realism or verisimilitude of the New Testament Gospels. Do they reflect what we know of early first-century Jewish Palestine? How do the New Testament Gospels compare to other Gospels and gospel-like writings from the second century? After all, if we expect to find a fair portrait of the historical Jesus in the New Testament Gospels, these writings should reflect his world, as reflected in other sources, in archaeological findings, and in the geography and topography of the land itself. The *fourth* question inquires into the nature of the discrepancies that we find in the New Testament Gospels. Why is John so different from the three Synoptic Gospels (Matthew,

Mark, and Luke)? Why are there discrepancies among the Synoptic Gospels, which otherwise overlap so much? What should we make of these discrepancies? And I will interrupt myself and express appreciation for Bart's paper because it laid out so many examples that now we can presuppose as I work through this. Are these discrepancies evidence of poor memory, deception, carelessness, or something else? Let us now turn to the first question.

How Good Are the Gospels? How Do They Compare with Other Writings?

One way of measuring the historical worth of the New Testament Gospels is to compare them with other writings, on which modern historians rely. Allow me to mention a number of these writings, beginning with the oldest. Most of my examples are historical works, which makes for a more appropriate comparison with the New Testament Gospels.

Herodotus of Halicarnassus (ca. 488–428 BC) wrote a work called *History*. The oldest major manuscript dates to AD 800, some twelve hundred years removed from the original.[3] Thucydides of Athens (ca. 460–400 BC) wrote a work called *History of the War*, meaning the Peloponnesian War between Athens and Sparta (431–404 BC). Our oldest major manuscript dates to AD 900.[4] Julius Caesar (100–44 BC) wrote his *Gallic War* during the years 58–50 BC. We possess some ten fairly well-preserved manuscripts, of which the oldest date to about AD 850.[5] Titus Livius, or simply Livy (59 BC to AD 17), authored *Roman History*. Of the original 142 books, only books 1–10 and 21–45 survive. Our oldest manuscript, containing parts of books 3–6, dates to about AD 350.[6] Our

---

3. See C. Hude, *Herodoti Historiae*, vol. 1, 3rd ed. (Oxford: Clarendon Press, 1927), vi–xi.
4. See H. S. Jones, *Thucydidis Historiae*, vol. 1, rev. ed. (Oxford: Clarendon Press, 1942), i–vi, ix–x.
5. See H. J. Edwards, *Caesar: The Gallic Wars*, LCL (Cambridge, MA: Harvard University Press, 1917), xvii–xviii. Most mss. are from the 11th and 12th centuries.
6. See R. S. Conway and C. F. Walters, *Titi Livi Ab urbe condita*, vol. 1, rev. ed. (Oxford: Clarendon Press, 1955), v–xxxix.

largest manuscript, containing most of what is extant, dates to the fifth century. Cornelius Tacitus (ca. AD 56–ca. 129) wrote *Histories* sometime around AD 110 and *Annals* sometime around AD 115. The latter may never have been completed. Portions of both are lost. Our oldest manuscripts date to the ninth and eleventh centuries AD. His minor works *Agricola* and *Germania* are preserved in a tenth-century codex.[7] Arrian (ca. AD 86–160) wrote the *Anabasis of Alexander* some 450 years after the brief reign of the famous conqueror. Our earliest extant copy of Arrian's work, which is damaged and in places illegible, dates to AD 1200.[8]

Against the backdrop of these classical works, the New Testament Gospels compare quite favorably. Large portions of the four Gospels are preserved in Papyrus 45, a papyrus codex that dates to the early third century, perhaps the late second century, as some contend. Late second-century Papyrus 66 preserves most of the Gospel of John. Late second-century Papyrus 75 preserves large chunks of Luke and John. A number of small fragments are candidates for a second-century date. These include Papyri 64/67, 77, 103, and 104, which preserve fragments of Matthew; Papyrus 4 (possibly part of Papyrus 64/67), which preserves a fragment of Luke; and Papyri 5, 52, 90, 108, and 109, which preserve small fragments of the Gospel of John. Not everyone dates these to the second century; some put them in the third. The prize for being the oldest fragment of a New Testament writing goes to Papyrus 52, which is dated by most scholars on papyri as sometime before AD 150.[9]

---

7. For the ms. evidence of *Histories*, see C. H. Moore, *Tacitus I: The Histories, Books I–III*, LCL (New York: G. P. Putnam's Sons, 1925), xiv. For the ms. evidence of *Annals*, see C. H. Moore, *Tacitus II: The Histories, Books IV–V; Annals, Books I–III*, LCL (New York: G. P. Putnam's Sons, 1931), 238–39.

8. See P. A. Brunt, trans., *Arrian: Anabasis of Alexander, Books I–IV*, LCL 236 (Cambridge, MA: Harvard University Press, 1976), xiv–xv. The ms. is Vienna Codex A, preserved in the Austrian National Library. Scholars make use of a 15th-century ms. to correct the older Vienna codex.

9. Papyrus 52 dates before AD 150, but not much before. Efforts to date Papyrus 52 to 120, perhaps even to 100, seem based more on apologetics than on paleography. On this point, see B. Nongbri, "Use and Abuse of $\mathfrak{P}^{52}$: Papyrological Pitfalls in the Dating of the Fourth Gospel," *HTR* 98 (2005): 23–52; P. Foster, "Bold Claims, Wishful Thinking, and Lessons about Dating Manuscripts from Papyrus Egerton 2," in *The World of Jesus and the Early Church*, ed. C. A. Evans (Peabody, MA: Hendrickson Publishers, 2011), 193–211. On the general question of how early New Testament papyri should be dated, see R. S. Bagnall, *Early Christian Books in Egypt* (Princeton, NJ: Princeton University Press, 2009), 1–49.

There are some fifty manuscripts that date before AD 300. Of course, we have the great Codex Sinaiticus and Codex Vaticanus, which contain the four Gospels, minus some well-known glosses (such as Mark's Ending [16:9–20] and John's story of the woman caught in the act of adultery [7:53–8:11]). These codices are dated to about AD 340.[10] This means that we have the complete text of the four New Testament Gospels preserved in documents about 270–280 years removed from the autographs, that we have substantial portions of the text of the Gospels preserved in documents about 130–200 years removed from the autographs, and that we have tiny portions of the text in perhaps as many as one dozen documents about 70–120 years removed from the autographs. All in all, this is not a bad record.[11] Compared to many of the classical writings and histories, where in most cases there are gaps of 800 to 1,000 years or more between the time of the author and our oldest surviving copy of his manuscript, it is an excellent record indeed.

The temporal distance between events of the history or historical personage and its record is also impressive. The Synoptic Gospels were written about 40 years or so after the death of Jesus (of course, proposed dates for the Gospels vary among scholars). The Fourth Gospel was written 60–70 years after the death of Jesus. In the case of some of the classical writers, the temporal distance is comparable. Indeed, some classical writers were eyewitnesses of at least some of the events they describe; others claimed acquaintance with eyewitnesses. But this is not always the case. Livy and Tacitus wrote greatly removed in time from most of the events they describe in their respective accounts of

---

10. K. Aland and B. Aland, eds., *The Text of the New Testament* (Grand Rapids: Wm. B. Eerdmans Publishing Co., 1987), 106–7; Bruce M. Metzger and Bart Ehrman, *The Text of the New Testament: Its Transmission, Corruption, and Restoration*, 4th ed. (New York: Oxford University Press, 2005), 62, 68; F. G. Kenyon, *The Text of the Greek Bible*, 3rd ed., ed. A. W. Adams (London: Duckworth, 1975), 78, 85: "Early fourth century" (for both Sinaiticus and Vaticanus). For weighty arguments in favor of dating Sinaiticus and Vaticanus to just before AD 340, see T. C. Skeat, "The Codex Sinaiticus[,] the Codex Vaticanus[,] and Constantine," *JTS* 50 (1999): 583–625.

11. See E. J. Epp, "Are Early New Testament Manuscripts Truly Abundant?," in *Israel's God and Rebecca's Children: Christology and Community in Early Judaism and Christianity; Essays in Honor of Larry W. Hurtado and Alan F. Segal*, ed. D. B. Capes, A. D. DeConick, H. K. Bond, and T. A. Miller (Waco, TX: Baylor University Press, 2007), 77–107; on 104, Epp counts 63 mss. at or before AD 300, opining that "the raw quantity of early manuscripts is sizable."

Roman history.[12] It is notable too that the work of Arrian, who wrote centuries after the death of Alexander the Great, is "marred by demonstrable errors and misunderstandings."[13] Arrian's problem is that he is not only distant from the events he describes; he is also distant from his earlier sources.[14]

As historical sources the New Testament Gospels look very promising. Three of the four Gospels were written before the end of the generation that knew Jesus or heard stories and teachings from those who knew him. This fact leaves open the possibility that their accounts can give us reliable and fair portraits of the life and teaching of Jesus.

The text of these Gospels is fully extant in manuscripts 250 years or so removed in time from the originals, and it is partially extant in several manuscripts much closer in time. This fact calls for a presumption that we have something rather close to the original text of the Gospels.[15] At this point we may ask, How were these manuscripts copied, and what did early Christians do with them? To these and related questions I now turn.

---

12. On this point, see M. I. Finley, *Ancient History: Evidence and Models* (New York: Penguin Books, 1985), 8–9.

13. A. B. Bosworth, "Arrian," in *The Oxford Classical Dictionary*, ed. S. Hornblower and A. Spawforth, 3rd ed. (New York: Oxford University Press, 1996), 175–76. See the similar judgment in *The Hellenistic Period and the Empire*, part 4 of vol. 1 of *The Cambridge History of Classical Literature*, ed. P. E. Easterling and B. M. W. Knox (Cambridge: Cambridge University Press, 1989), 145: "Mistakes of this sort, and omissions or deficiencies on other topics, limit the value of the [*Anabasis of Alexander*] as history."

14. The "earlier" sources are not as early as we could wish. Arrian's earliest sources are from the first century BC, or about 300 years after Alexander's death (see the next footnote). Historians believe that eyewitness testimony is found in these sources, however well or poorly it was handed down. Despite the numerous problems, Brunt (*Arrian*, xvi) says, "Arrian unquestionably provides us with the best evidence we have for Alexander." On the manuscript tradition, see Brunt, *Arrian*, xvi–xxxiv.

15. I say "rather close" because unless we find the autographs themselves, we will never possess, strictly speaking, the original text. On this important point, see D. C. Parker, *The Living Text of the Gospels* (Cambridge: Cambridge University Press, 1997), as well as some of his essays. Among these I suggest Parker, "Et incarnatus est," *SJT* 54 (2001): 330–43. However, the admission that we do not possess the original text, in its precise autographic form, does not justify the excessive skepticism voiced by Bart D. Ehrman in some of his recent publications and public talks and interviews. See the reviews of Ehrman's *Misquoting Jesus: The Story behind Who Changed the Bible and Why* (San Francisco: HarperOne, 2005), such as by D. B. Wallace, "The Gospel according to Bart: A Review Article of *Misquoting Jesus* by Bart Ehrman," *JETS* 49 (2006): 327–49, https://www.etsjets.org/files/JETS-PDFs/49/49-2/JETS_49-2_327-349_Wallace.pdf; J. E. Komoszewski, M. J. Sawyer, and D. B. Wallace, *Reinventing Jesus* (Grand Rapids: Kregel Publications, 2006), 53–117; D. B. Wallace, "How Badly Did the Early Scribes Corrupt the New Testament? An Examination of Bart Ehrman's Claims," in *Contending with Christianity's Critics: Answering New Atheists and Other Objectors*, ed. P. Copan and W. L. Craig (Nashville: B&H Publishing, 2009), 148–66. Several recent scholarly studies have concluded that the early Christian scribes were competent. See J. R. Royse, *Scribal Habits in Early Greek New Testament Papyri*, NTTSD 36 (Leiden: Brill, 2008); A. Mugridge, *Copying Early Christian Texts: A Study of Scribal Practice*, WUNT 362 (Tübingen: Mohr Siebeck, 2016). Mugridge describes Christian scribes as "competent" and "experienced."

Writing, Copying, and Studying Books in Late Antiquity

Nearly a half million documents were recovered from rubbish heaps on the outskirts of the ancient city of Oxyrhynchus in southern Egypt, a few miles west of the Nile River and about 200 kilometers southwest of modern Cairo.[16] Only a small portion of this rich trove of mostly papyri has been published to date.[17] New Testament writings, as well as other writings, have garnered most of the attention. And outside the New Testament itself a very well-known gospel is the *Gospel of Thomas*.

One of the important finds at Oxyrhynchus and at a few other sites has been the discovery of libraries or collections of related books and documents that were thrown out together. In a recent study George Houston plausibly argues that, in each case, the evidence suggests that someone in antiquity "was clearing texts, old or no longer wanted, out of his library, and had them taken out together and thrown on the dump. Support for the possibility of coherent collections being preserved in dumps comes from the large numbers of similar bodies of documentary materials, in which specific names and dates often prove that the papyri in the concentration belonged together and came from a single original archive."[18]

Houston reviews more than fifty such collections or libraries.[19] The number of books and documents in these collections

---

16. For a scholarly overview of the find, see A. K. Bowman et al., eds., *Oxyrhynchus: A City and Its Texts*, Graeco-Roman Memoirs 93 (London: Egypt Exploration Society, 2007).

17. I am grateful to Daniela Colomo and the staff in the Sackler Library (part of the Bodleian complex in Oxford) for showing me box after box of yet-to-be-published papyri from Oxyrhynchus.

18. G. W. Houston, "Papyrological Evidence for Book Collections and Libraries in the Roman Empire," in *Ancient Literacies: The Culture of Reading in Greece and Rome*, ed. W. A. Johnson and H. N. Parker (New York: Oxford University Press, 2009), 233–67, here 247, n. 42; Houston, *Inside Roman Libraries: Book Collections and Their Management in Antiquity*, Studies in the History of Greece and Rome (Chapel Hill: University of North Carolina Press, 2014), 120–21, 175–76. For more on the general topic of collections and archives, see K. Vandorpe, "Archives and Dossiers," in *The Oxford Handbook of Papyrology*, ed. R. S. Bagnall (Oxford: Oxford University Press, 2009), 216–55. Houston's study is concerned with libraries, that is, collections largely made up of literary works, whereas Vandorpe's broader study mostly takes into account collections of business papers and records.

19. See the tables in Houston, "Papyrological Evidence," 238–39, 249–50, 252–54. In the first table Houston lists eight collections: three from Arsinoite, two from Oxyrhynchus, one from Apollinopolis Magna, one from Hermapolis Magna, and one from Memphis. In the second table Houston lists another ten collections: six from Oxyrhynchus, one from Antinoopolis, one from Aphrodito, one from Herculaneum, and one from Karanis. The third table comes from B. Grenfell and A. S. Hunt's "great find" at Oxyrhynchus during the winter 1905–6 season. In all, Houston lists and describes 53

range from as few as twenty to as many as one thousand. Most range in date from the second century BC to the third century AD (a couple of collections are a bit later). Some of the collections are specialized libraries; some seem to be general collections. Most of the collections, including those that are highly specialized and scholarly, include some light reading, such as novels. The highly specialized libraries include works on philosophy, medicine, grammar, commentaries, glossaries, and drafts of works in various stages of completion. Most of the manuscripts were prepared by professional scribes; many of these manuscripts were proofread by the original scribe and then by a second scribe called a *diorthōtēs*.[20] These professionally prepared manuscripts are book rolls (scrolls), not codices (bound like books today). Many books in a given collection were penned by the same scribe.

Most of these collections had been in possession of affluent people, though in some cases we see evidence of economy (such as writing on the back side, or the *verso*). Many of these manuscripts give evidence of being carefully studied. The texts are glossed and corrected and sometimes are accompanied with exegetical notes.[21] There is evidence that readers compared duplicate texts and engaged in what we today call textual criticism.[22] I am not talking about Christian materials here; these are non-Christian libraries I am describing.

Perhaps the biggest surprise has been the discovery of how long these manuscripts were in use before being retired.

---

collections. Note that Houston excludes religious libraries (Christian, gnostic, Manichean). For further discussion of the Herculaneum library, preserved by the hot volcanic ash of Vesuvius in AD 79, see D. Sider, "The Special Case of Herculaneum," in Bagnall, *Oxford Handbook of Papyrology*, 303–19.

20. See K. Haines-Eitzen, *Guardians of Letters: Literacy, Power, and the Transmitters of Early Christian Literature* (Oxford: Oxford University Press, 2000), 85–87. Many scribes reread and corrected their own work. This is seen in the case of the scribe who wrote out Papyrus 66. He reread his work and made some 450 corrections, which demonstrated his commitment to getting it right. See Royse, *Scribal Habits*, 502–4; Haines-Eitzen, *Guardians of Letters*, 109.

21. See the third table in Houston, "Papyrological Evidence," 252–54.

22. An obvious example is collection 14 in the third list: see Houston, "Papyrological Evidence," 252; and on 258 we find that Herodotus, book 3, is "carefully written and then annotated by at least two nearly contemporary hands, who provided variants and, perhaps, explanatory notes." Houston comments that about 45 percent of the books in this collection have marginal notes, often indicating variant readings. On this point, see also the general comment in E. G. Turner, "Scribes and Scholars," in Bowman et al., *Oxyrhynchus*, 256–61, here 259–60.

Houston finds that manuscripts were in use anywhere from 150 to 500 years, with the average usually 200 to 300 years.[23] Almost all of these libraries and collections were multigenerational, being handed down to descendants or in some cases purchased in their entirety by a new family or collector.

What does this all this mean for our understanding of the literature of the New Testament? First of all, it gives us some insight into how literature in late antiquity was collected, read, studied, and copied. It suggests that those interested in literature saw the need for comparison of texts, in recognition of scribal errors and textual corruption of one sort or another. It also shows that manuscripts were in use for a very long time.

I want to pursue that point a bit further. If manuscripts were in use for two or three centuries before their destruction or retirement, we must entertain the possibility, perhaps even probability, that the autographs and first copies of first-century New Testament writings continued to circulate, to be studied, and to be copied on through the second century and, in some cases, perhaps even into the third century. This means that the original copy of the Gospel of Matthew, let us suppose written and first circulated in AD 75, may actually have remained in use until the time when Papyrus 45 was copied. If so, we should assume that the autograph of Matthew would have exerted influence on the text of Matthew, at least in the region in which it circulated, throughout the time of its existence and circulation. This means that second-generation copies of Matthew could have been produced as late as the end of the second century and beginning of the third—if George Houston's findings are taken seriously and not simply ignored or gratuitously declared to be irrelevant.[24]

---

23. Houston, "Papyrological Evidence," 248–51; Houston, *Inside Roman Libraries*, 120–21.

24. Houston's findings may support Tertullian's claim that in his time (late second century) some of the "authentic" (*authenticae*) writings (autographs?) of Paul were still available for examination (cf. Tertullian, *Prescription against Heretics* 36). The *Oxford Latin Dictionary* defines *authenticum* as "an original document, autograph." For discussion of this passage, see D. L. Bock and D. B. Wallace, *Dethroning Jesus* (Nashville: Thomas Nelson, 2007), 45–46; as well as a paper by D. B. Wallace, "Did the Original New Testament Manuscripts Still Exist in the Second Century?" (2009; published only online, https://bible.org/article/did-original-new-testament-manuscripts-still-exist-second-century-0). It has been suggested that Tertullian's term *authenticae* refers to the Greek instead of the Latin, or to unabridged, unmutilated versions of the apostolic writings. I agree with Wallace that "originals" or "autographs" is the most natural sense of *authenticae*. Wallace also draws our attention to an

But more needs to be said about the longevity of autographic manuscripts. We usually assume a single autograph per New Testament writing. I am not saying papyrologists assume this to be so, but I think many Christians and seminarians assume such. But that can hardly have been the case. No one produces a single exemplar of a work and then circulates it. This is well documented in the papyri, especially with reference to letters.[25] An "autograph" is produced by a scribe; the author of the letter signs it in his own hand, usually along with a greeting;[26] and then the scribe makes a second copy, which is retained for the author's records.[27] In the case of some letters, such as circular letters, several signed autographs may have been prepared.

If there were in fact two or more originals, or autographs, of the New Testament writings, as we should assume, then the chances improve that some of these autographs survived as long as many of the manuscripts that papyrologists have found in the aforementioned discarded libraries and collections. In other words, we may have an overlap in the lifetime of the autograph and the copies we now possess in libraries and museums. Now we turn to our third question.

Do the New Testament Gospels Exhibit Verisimilitude?

An important test for a document that we think may provide us with historical data is the question of verisimilitude, a

---

early fourth-century statement by Peter, Bishop of Alexandria (d. AD 311), who speaks of the autograph of the Gospel of John: "The autograph copy itself of the evangelist John, which up to this day has by divine grace been preserved in the most holy church of Ephesus, . . . is there adored by the faithful" (frag. 5.2). See A. Roberts and J. Donaldson, eds., *The Ante-Nicene Fathers*, 10 vols. (Edinburgh: T&T Clark, 1898), 6:283. Given the longevity of mss., the Bishop of Alexandria could well have been correct.

25. Multiple copies of documents are dispatched "in triplicate" (P.Oxy. 1278) or "in quadruplicate" (P.Lond. 978). This language is echoed in Eusebius, when in reference to the fifty copies of Scripture commissioned by Emperor Constantine, he refers to copies being "dispatched in batches of three and four." On this point, see Skeat, "The Codex Sinaiticus," 607–9.

26. On the autographic features in letters of late antiquity and their relevance for understanding the letters of Paul, see J. A. D. Weima, *Neglected Endings: The Significance of the Pauline Letter Closings*, JSNTSup 101 (Sheffield: Sheffield Academic Press, 1994), 118–35.

27. J. Murphy-O'Connor, *Paul the Letter-Writer: His World, His Options, His Skills* (Collegeville, MN: Liturgical Press, 1995), 12.

likeness to reality as we know it from the past.[28] That is, does the document in question match with what we know of the place, people, and period described? Do the contents of the document cohere with what is known through other written sources and through archaeological finds? Do the contents of the document give evidence of acquaintance with the topography and geography of the region that forms the backdrop to the story? Does the author of the document exhibit knowledge of the culture and customs of the people he describes? These are the kinds of questions historians ask of documents.[29]

The New Testament Gospels and Acts exhibit a great deal of verisimilitude.[30] They speak of real people (e.g., Pontius Pilate, Herod Antipas, Annas, Caiaphas, et al.) and real events. They refer to real places. They speak of real customs, institutions, offices, and beliefs. Jesus' engagement with his contemporaries, both supporters and opponents, reflects an understanding of Old Testament Scripture and theology current in pre-70 Jewish Palestine—as we now know, thanks to the Dead Sea Scrolls.

In contrast to the verisimilitude of the New Testament Gospels and Acts, the second-century Gospels and gospel-like writings, such as the gnostic Gospels and Syria's *Gospel of Thomas*, do not exhibit verisimilitude. On the basis of *Gospel of Thomas* alone, would we know that Jesus was Jewish? Would we have any sense of his message? Any sense of his travels, of his itinerary? Any sense of life in first-century Jewish Palestine? Even in the case of the *Gospel of Peter*, a second-century text that heavily

---

28. On the importance of verisimilitude in historical research, see L. Gottschalk, "The Historian and the Historical Document," in *The Use of Personal Documents in History, Anthropology, and Sociology*, by L. Gottschalk, C. Kluckhorn, and R. Angell, Bulletin 53 (New York: Social Science Research Council, 1945), 35–38. Gottschalk equates verisimilitude with credibility.

29. Archaeologists and historians ask if there is a correlation between text and realia. If there is such correspondence, then we may speak of verisimilitude. The point has been well stated by R. S. Hendel, "Giants at Jericho," *BAR* 35, no. 2 (2009): 20, 66: "Biblical archaeology . . . involves the rigorous correlation of textual data from the Bible and material evidence from archaeology." It is to this principle that Sherwin-White alludes, when he says: "The basic reason for this confidence is, if put summarily, the existence of external confirmations." A. N. Sherwin-White, *Roman Society and Roman Law* (Oxford: Clarendon Press, 1963), 186–87. The historical and geographical verisimilitude of the canonical Gospels was long ago noted by Henry Thayer in his 1895 Society of Biblical Literature presidential address. See J. H. Thayer, "The Historical Element in the New Testament," *JBL* 14 (1895): 1–18, esp. 15.

30. I bring Acts into the discussion at this point because it, like the four Gospels, describes persons and events in first-century Jewish Palestine.

relies on Matthew, there are glaring lapses of verisimilitude. This author apparently doesn't know who governs Jerusalem or Judea. Is it Pilate, or is it Herod Antipas? This uninformed author thinks that Jewish elders would spend the night at a Jewish cemetery, to keep watch over the tomb of Jesus.

Unlike the second-century Gospels, the first-century New Testament Gospels and Acts exhibit the kind of verisimilitude we should expect of writings written within a generation of their principal figure, that is, writings significantly informed by eyewitness tradition. We find linguistic verisimilitude, and by this I mean Hebrew and Aramaic traces in what are otherwise Greek writings. We find geographic and topographic verisimilitude, cultural and archaeological verisimilitude, as well as religious, economic, and social verisimilitude. We find impressive overlap with other texts from this time period, such as the writings of Josephus and the aforementioned Dead Sea Scrolls and related writings.[31]

The verisimilitude of the New Testament Gospels and Acts is such that historians and archaeologists regularly make use of them. I can illustrate this claim by directing you to a recently published book titled *Jesus and Archaeology*,[32] a book that grew out of a conference in Israel, which offered the usual learned papers but also included on-site visits and examinations of archaeological excavations. The volume includes thirty-one essays. A third of the contributors are Jewish, and about a third are trained archaeologists. The remainder are historians and biblical scholars. If you turn to the index in the back of the book, you will find more than one thousand references to the New Testament Gospels and Acts. There are very few references to the second-century extracanonical writings, and not one of these references has anything to do with historical

---

31. The Dead Sea Scrolls and archaeological excavations (esp. of inscribed ossuaries) in Israel have demonstrated that Hebrew, Aramaic, and Greek were in use there in the first century. This linguistic reality is shown in the four Gospels, as we should expect, if they authentically reflect the world of Jesus. On this point, see R. H. Gundry, "The Language Milieu of First-Century Palestine: Its Bearing on the Authenticity of the Gospel Tradition," *JBL* 83 (1964): 404–8.

32. J. H. Charlesworth, ed., *Jesus and Archaeology* (Grand Rapids: Wm. B. Eerdmans Publishing Co., 2006).

verisimilitude.[33] If the New Testament Gospels and Acts were little better than the second-century extracanonical writings, then their extensive usage by historians and archaeologists would be difficult to explain.

As it turns out, no explanation is required. Historians and archaeologists rightly regard the New Testament writings as early and generally reliable. I am not saying that they think the canonical Gospels are inerrant; that's not what I am claiming. I am not saying that they think they are free of mistakes; I am not saying that. What I am saying is that many of these scholars do see Matthew, Mark, Luke, John, and Acts as valuable sources, without which historical and archaeological work in this field of studies and this period of time would be much more difficult. No archaeologist or historian would say this with regard to the *Gospel of Peter*, the *Gospel of Thomas*, or most of the other second-century writings, which some New Testament scholars and popular writers in recent years have lionized and sensationalized.

The New Testament Gospels may contain useful historical data, but they also contain a number of discrepancies, as Professor Ehrman has shared with us. Why do they? Do discrepancies discredit the Gospels? To these questions we now turn.

The Meaning of Differences and Discrepancies

Any careful, fair reading of the Gospels, side by side, the horizontal reading—that's the exact language I use with my

---

33. Other works can be cited that make this point. See E. M. Meyers, ed., *Galilee through the Centuries: Confluence of Cultures*, Duke Judaic Studies 1 (Winona Lake, IN: Eisenbrauns, 1999). There are more than 300 citations from the canonical Gospels and Acts and another 150 citations from the writings of Josephus, but not one citation from one of the second-century noncanonical Gospels. The essays in this book (Meyers, *Galilee*), which deals with history and archaeology, refer to the New Testament Gospels and other writings because they exhibit verisimilitude and aid research. For additional examples of studies concerned with the world of Jesus, in which the New Testament Gospels and Acts are frequently cited and the second-century Gospels are rarely cited, if at all, see also S. Freyne, *Galilee and Gospel: Collected Essays*, WUNT 125 (Tübingen: Mohr Siebeck, 2000); M. A. Chancey, *The Myth of a Gentile Galilee*, SNTSMS 118 (Cambridge: Cambridge University Press, 2002); Chancey, *Greco-Roman Culture and the Galilee of Jesus*, SNTSMS 134 (Cambridge: Cambridge University Press, 2005); C. A. Evans, *Jesus and His World: The Archaeological Evidence* (Louisville, KY: Westminster John Knox Press, 2012).

students too—will reveal these differences and discrepancies.[34] Some of these discrepancies are more apparent than real, but many of them are indeed real. We observe differences in the wording of Jesus' teachings that are clustered together in one Gospel (for example, in a Matthean discourse) but scattered over several chapters in another Gospel (such as Luke's Central Section, chapters 10–18). The order and sequence of several episodes sometimes vary from one Gospel to another. Details in parallel stories sometimes vary; and on it goes.

Most scholars are not troubled by these discrepancies, recognizing several factors involved. In fact, many Gospel commentators revel in the differences, for differences are often indicators of interpretive and theological nuances that provide clues as to the respective evangelists' strategies and purposes for writing. Although the Matthean evangelist likes what he has found in the Gospel of Mark and so incorporates about 90 percent of it, he does not hesitate to make revisions. By supplementing the Markan narrative with additional teaching, by adding a number of fulfillment quotations, and by doing some old-fashioned editing, Matthew shows how Jesus is not in fact a lawbreaker but a fulfiller of the law; Jesus is a figure greater than Moses and teaches the true way of righteousness, a figure who is wiser than Solomon, and a figure who is a king greater than David. The evangelist Luke also appreciates the Gospel of Mark, but his purpose for writing is very different from Matthew's. Luke augments, rearranges, and edits material inherited from Mark and elsewhere, all in an effort to show, among other things, that what God has accomplished in Jesus is of profound significance for all people and not just for Israel. In presenting the teaching of Jesus in this new light, the evangelist Luke prepares for his second volume, the book of Acts, which recounts the birth of the church and its evangelistic outreach to Israel and the Roman Empire.

But it wasn't only the evangelists who edited the teachings and stories of Jesus. So did Jesus' earliest followers, long before

---

34. In the words of Bart D. Ehrman, *Jesus, Interrupted: Revealing the Hidden Contradictions in the Bible (and Why We Don't Know about Them)* (San Francisco: HarperOne, 2009), 21: "Reading the Gospels horizontally [i.e., side by side] reveals all sorts of differences and discrepancies."

the Gospels were written. Gospel scholars are convinced that the tradition inherited by the evangelists had been edited to one degree or another.[35] In other words, the earliest recitation of the words and deeds of Jesus was not static or frozen; it was a living, adaptable tradition. Scholars familiar with the pedagogy of late antiquity—in both Jewish as well as Greco-Roman circles—know this and are not troubled by it. But I suspect that many conservative Christians—especially those of a fundamentalist stripe, and perhaps some here—may not know this and may view the editing and adapting of the Jesus tradition with misgivings, including the discrepancies that Professor Ehrman has outlined, and he could have added many more such.

The "discrepancies" in the Gospels begin with Jesus himself. His teaching was not static and unchanging. It was adaptable, situational, applied to a variety of settings, and altered as the occasion required. He taught his disciples accordingly. Yes, they were to learn his teaching, to memorize his words,[36] but they were expected to apply them according to the needs of evangelism and teaching. These disciples, or "learners" (both the Greek *mathētai* and the Hebrew *talmîdîm* mean "learners"), could hardly claim to be genuine disciples if their learning never progressed beyond rote memory and mere repetition.

How do we know this? We know it because this was the understanding of education and pedagogy in late antiquity—in both Jewish and Greco-Roman society. Jewish and Greco-Roman pedagogies were not separate and isolated from one another. Most of the rabbinic rules of exegesis were learned from the Greeks. Greek and Jewish memory techniques and

---

35. This has been the principal insight of form criticism. For the classic statement in English scholarship, see Vincent Taylor, *The Formation of the Gospel Tradition* (London: Macmillan, 1935).

36. For recent studies of the role of memory in Jewish and Greek education in late antiquity and the relevance it may have for understanding the transmission of the teaching of Jesus, see A. D. Baum, *Der mündliche Faktor und seine Bedeutung für die synoptische Frage: Analogien aus der antiken Literatur, der Experimentalpsychologie, der Oral Poetry-Forschung und dem rabbinischen Traditionswesen*, Texte und Arbeiten zum neutestamentlichen Zeitalter 49 (Tübingen: Francke Verlag, 2008); R. K. McIver, *Memory, Jesus, and the Synoptic Gospels*, SBLRBS (Atlanta: Society of Biblical Literature, 2011). Baum makes a compelling case for the memorization of the whole of the Jesus tradition, but his argument that there is no literary relationship among the Synoptic Gospels is not convincing. McIver, especially concerned with pedagogy and eyewitness tradition, takes into account population and longevity of first-century Palestinian Jews. He finds it probable that a significant number of eyewitnesses were still living when the Synoptic Gospels were composed. See McIver, *Memory, Jesus*, esp. 202–9.

practice overlapped. Techniques of argumentation overlapped. Scribal practices overlapped.[37]

Young Greeks began their education by memorizing *chreiai*—brief anecdotes in which a well-known figure says or does something significant and of value.[38] As the student progressed, he learned to insert a *chreia* into his argument or to string together several *chreiai*, and in doing so he was free to edit the beginnings and endings of these *chreiai*. The student was not only permitted to edit these pithy anecdotes; he was also required to do so, for the sake of clarity. This point needs to be underscored: recitation of these anecdotes presupposed memorization, but memorization did not prohibit a change of wording, nor did it prohibit expansion or contraction,[39] so long as the change remained true to the original meaning and intent. The overarching concern was clarity.[40]

---

37. S. Lieberman, *Hellenism in Jewish Palestine: Studies in the Literary Transmission, Beliefs, and Manners of Palestine in the I Century B.C.E.—IV Century C.E.*, 2nd ed., TSJTSA 18 (New York: Jewish Theological Seminary of America, 1962), esp. 28–114. See also the older but still useful studies of D. Daube, "Rabbinic Methods of Interpretation and Hellenistic Rhetoric," *HUCA* 12 (1949): 239–64; Daube, "Alexandrian Methods of Interpretation and the Rabbis," in *Essays in Greco-Roman and Related Talmudic Literature*, ed. H. Fischel (New York: Krav, 1977), 165–82. For more current discussion, as well as a number of examples of *chreiai* in rabbinic writings, see A. J. Avery-Peck, "Rhetorical Argumentation in Early Rabbinic Pronouncement Stories," *Semeia* 64 (1994): 49–69; M. S. Jaffee, *Torah in the Mouth: Writing and Oral Tradition in Palestinian Judaism, 200 BCE–400 CE* (New York: Oxford University Press, 2001), esp. 126–52 and notes on 201–8.

38. For a convenient selection of texts in which the *chreia* is discussed, see G. A. Kennedy, *Progymnasmata: Greek Textbooks of Prose Composition and Rhetoric*, Writings from the Greco-Roman World 10 (Atlanta: Society of Biblical Literature, 2003), 15–23 (Theon of Alexandria), 76–77 (Hermogenes of Tarsus), 97–99 (Aphthonius of Antioch), 139–42 (Nicolaus of Myra), 193–96 (John of Sardis). For additional texts and commentary, see R. F. Hock and E. N. O'Neil, *The Progymnasmata*, vol. 1 of *The Chreia in Ancient Rhetoric*, SBLTT 27: Greco-Roman Religion Series 9 (Atlanta: Scholars Press, 1986). See also R. Webb, "The Progymnasmata as Practice," in *Education in Greek and Roman Antiquity*, ed. Yun Lee Too (Leiden: Brill, 2001), 289–316; D. B. Gowler, "The *Chreia*," in *The Historical Jesus in Context*, ed. A.-J. Levine, D. C. Allison Jr., and J. D. Crossan, Princeton Readings in Religion (Princeton, NJ: Princeton University Press, 2006), 132–48. For a list of *chreiai* in the early rabbis, see Avery-Peck, "Rhetorical Argumentation," 67.

39. See B. L. Mack, "Elaboration of the *Chreia* in the Hellenistic School," in *Patterns of Persuasion in the Gospels*, by B. L. Mack and V. K. Robbins, Foundations and Facets (Sonoma, CA: Polebridge Press, 1989), 31–67; Gowler, "The *Chreia*," 139. See Theon of Alexandria, *Progymnasmata* 101 (in *Rhetores Graeci*, ed. L. von Spengel [Leipzig: Teubner, 1853–56], vol. 2): "*Chreiai* are practiced by restatement, grammatical inflection, comment, and inversion, and we expand and compress the *chreia*. . . . Practice by restatement is self-evident; for we try to express the assigned *chreia*, as best we can, with the same words (as in the version given us) or with others in the clearest way." See Kennedy, *Progymnasmata*, 19.

40. On this point, see esp. S. Byrskog, "The Transmission of the Jesus Tradition: Old and New Insights," *Early Christianity* 1 (2010): 441–68, here 459; as well as Byrskog, "The Transmission of the Jesus Tradition," in *Handbook for Study of the Historical Jesus*, ed. S. E. Porter and T. Holmén, 4 vols. (Leiden: Brill, 2011), 2:1465–94, here 1492.

New Testament scholars have discovered the *chreia* form in the Gospels. This has been much discussed in the literature of the last twenty-five years or so.[41] As in the case of the *chreiai*, so in the Gospels we observe relatively stabilized units of tradition, often from Q (both Matthew and Luke tap into that hypothetical *Quelle*, "source," of Jesus' teaching), rearranged, expanded (usually with additional Q material), and introduced and contextualized in various ways. This editing, adapting, clustering, and contextualizing quite naturally created "discrepancies," and indeed they do. This always happens when we have overlapping accounts.

Helpful examples of such overlap may be found in the biographies and histories of the contemporaries Plutarch, Suetonius, and Tacitus, who give us accounts of various events and major figures, such as Roman emperors. Craig Keener has recently compared the various accounts of the life and death of Otho,[42] who for a brief time ruled as Rome's emperor (January 15 till April 16 of the year 69).[43] The three historians wrote forty to fifty years after the death of the would-be emperor. Thus the temporal distance between them and their subject is about the same as the temporal distance between the New Testament evangelists and their subject, Jesus of Nazareth.

The three Roman historians drew on some common material, just as the New Testament evangelists did. The principal elements in the story of Otho, as told by the three Roman historians, number about seventy, as Craig Keener has outlined them in his study. No one version of the man's life contains all seventy of these elements, but most of them are found in

---

41. J. R. Butts, "The *Chreia* in the Synoptic Gospels," *BTB* 16 (1986): 132–38; V. K. Robbins, "The *Chreia*," in *Greco-Roman Literature and the New Testament: Selected Forms and Genres*, ed. David E. Aune, SBL Sources for Biblical Study 21 (Atlanta: Scholars Press, 1988), 1–23; Robbins, "*Chreia* and Pronouncement Story in Synoptic Studies," in Mack and Robbins, *Patterns of Persuasion*, 1–29; J. H. Neyrey, "Questions, *Chreiai*, and Challenges to Honor: The Interface of Rhetoric and Culture in Mark's Gospel," *CBQ* 60 (1998): 657–81; S. Byrskog, "The Early Church as a Narrative Fellowship: An Exploratory Study of the Performance of the '*Chreia*,'" *TTKi* 78 (2007): 207–26.

42. C. S. Keener, "Otho: A Targeted Comparison of Suetonius' Biography and Tacitus' History, with Implications for the Gospels' Historical Reliability," *BBR* 21 (2011): 331–55.

43. Otho (AD 32–69), a friend of Nero, served as governor of Lusitania from 58 until Nero's death in 68. Initially he backed Galba as Nero's successor, but later had himself proclaimed emperor. Defeated in battle, he committed suicide.

Plutarch and Tacitus. Several are missing in Suetonius, for his is a much shorter account. In fact, Suetonius's compression of the story sometimes creates confusion. If it had not been for the fuller accounts of Plutarch and Tacitus, historians would often not be in a position to clear it up. And historians actually do need to "mash together" (as Ehrman sometimes puts it) these three accounts in order to come up with as complete and as accurate an account of Otho as we can achieve.

There are several discrepancies. Suetonius and Tacitus give Otho's astrologer different names. Perhaps this is due to confusing that name with the name of the astrologer for Vespasian, a later emperor. Tacitus says Densus defended Galba; Plutarch says Densus defended Galba's adopted son, Piso. Tacitus says Otho left the city of Rome in the care of his brother Titianus, but elsewhere Tacitus says Titianus had left Rome. Suetonius says Rome was under the authority of Sabinus. Some other discrepancies, including chronological ones, could be cited.[44] The function of rhetoric, including the practices associated with *chreiai*, can be detected throughout the accounts of the three Roman historians, especially as they relate to Otho's speeches. We observe expansion, condensation, omission, and rearrangement.

Discrepancies notwithstanding, the points of agreement are far more numerous. A coherent and plausible portrait of the life, brief reign, and death of Otho emerges. No historian despairs over the discrepancies and indications of authorial bias and declares, in the light of such bias and discrepancies, that we cannot know what Otho did and what happened to him.

The same applies to the New Testament Gospels. The stories and teachings of Jesus have been edited, contextualized in ways that lead to clarity. The teaching of Jesus has been applied in new ways and new insights as new questions and problems arose. All of this reflects the way Jesus taught his disciples. It shows the pedagogy of the time. The disciples were not tape recorders. They were disciples, trained to understand the

---

44. For many more examples, see Keener, "Otho," 338–51.

teaching of Jesus, not simply to repeat it word for word. They were trained to apply it as they gave leadership to the following of Jesus, a following that in time became known as the church.

It is to this training, this ability to apply Jesus' teaching in new and creative ways, that the saying in Matthew 13 may well apply: "Therefore every scribe who has been discipled [*mathēteutheis*] for the kingdom of heaven is like a householder who brings out of his treasure what is new and what is old" (v. 52). Jesus did not say, "Every scribe who has been discipled for the kingdom of heaven must repeat my words verbatim." Regarding this verse, Dale Allison and W. D. Davies, in their commentary on the Gospel of Matthew, rightly comment that "the ability to teach things new and old rests upon the ability to understand Jesus' teaching."[45] Precisely.

I believe that most Christians do not understand the genre and nature of biblical literature. When it comes to writings that are ostensibly "historical," broadly speaking, there is a tendency to impose upon them a modern understanding of what constitutes proper history. When someone is quoted, we expect the quotation to be verbatim and punctuated with quotation marks. We expect strict chronology and sequence. If sources are cited, we expect footnotes.

The Gospels reflect a world quite different from our own. Proper historiography in late antiquity allowed for and sometimes required editing and paraphrasing, always for the sake of clarification. This is what we see in the Gospels. In the New Testament Gospels we find a plausible portrait of the historical Jesus, a portrait that is true to what we know of the time in which Jesus and his disciples lived.[46] Major New Testament scholars, who do not identify themselves as conservative Christians (and here I can name John Meier, Ben Meyer, and

---

45. D. C. Allison Jr. and W. D. Davies, *Commentary on Matthew VIII–XVIII*, vol. 2 of *A Critical and Exegetical Commentary on the Gospel according to Saint Matthew*, ICC (Edinburgh: T&T Clark, 1991), 448.
46. Another helpful way of putting it is by A. Le Donne, *The Historiographical Jesus: Memory, Typology, and the Son of David* (Waco, TX: Baylor University Press, 2009), 268: "The historical Jesus is the memorable Jesus; he is the one who set refraction trajectories in motion and who set the initial parameters for how his memories were to be interpreted by his contemporaries."

E. P. Sanders, among others), believe that the Gospels are more than adequate as sources from which we may construct a portrait of the historical Jesus. In the introduction to his critically acclaimed *Jesus and Judaism*, Sanders remarks: "The dominant view today seems to be that we can know pretty well what Jesus was out to accomplish, that we can know a lot about what he said, and those two things make sense within the world of first-century Judaism."[47] What Professor Sanders has said was true in 1985, when he published that book, and it is just as true today. If historical-Jesus scholars did not really think the Gospels could give us this kind of information, then we wouldn't even bother with this particular topic: we would go on to other things. Thank you very much.

BART EHRMAN: RESPONSE

Well, thank you very much. And thank you, Craig, for that very stimulating and learned talk. I think the most astounding thing—I don't know if the rest of you picked up on this—is that we are not disagreeing very much. (I should say that in some of my debates, I really don't like the other guy. That is not the case here, I am happy to say.) Let's begin by recalling the topic: "Can we trust the Bible on the historical Jesus?" I think that the answer is no for reasons that I have given. I want to deal with several of the points that Craig made and again thereby affirm that, in terms of the content of what he said,

---

47. E. P. Sanders, *Jesus and Judaism* (Philadelphia: Fortress Press, 1985), 2. Every bit as optimistic is B. F. Meyer, *The Aims of Jesus* (London: SCM Press, 1979), 19: "The immediate aim of the present work . . . is to understand the Jesus of ancient Palestine." Meyer believes this aim has been achieved. See his conclusion on pp. 223–53. I might also mention Armand Puig i Tàrrech, *Jesus: A Biography* (Waco, TX: Baylor University Press, 2011). Puig i Tàrrech is Dean and Professor of New Testament on the Faculty of Theology of the University of Catalonia in Barcelona. Currently he is president of the Society of New Testament Studies, an elite international society of New Testament scholars, whose membership is by vetting and invitation only. He has the highest regard for the historical accuracy of the Gospels. One might also wish to consider the conclusion regarding Jesus' self-understanding reached by D. C. Allison Jr., *Constructing Jesus: Memory, Imagination, and History* (Grand Rapids: Baker Academic, 2010), 221–304. Allison very plausibly concludes that the Christology that the early church embraced (which understood Jesus in divine terms) is rooted in the historical Jesus, just as the New Testament Gospels portray. The same conclusion is reached in S. Grindheim, *God's Equal: What Can We Know about Jesus' Self-Understanding in the Synoptic Gospels?*, LNTS 446 (New York: T&T Clark, 2011).

I disagree with very little. There are a couple of issues, though, that I think are important to stress.

The first major point that Craig made throughout a good deal of his talk is that the Gospels of the New Testament are better attested in ancient manuscripts than other ancient writings. The New Testament is better attested in ancient manuscripts than Herodotus, Thucydides, Julius Caesar, and Livy, and so on. That is absolutely right. I completely agree with it. I also think that it is irrelevant to the topic.

The topic is "Can we trust the Bible on the historical Jesus?" It is irrelevant whether we know what the authors of the NT originally wrote or not. The ancient manuscripts, the ones that Craig was describing at some great length, are used in order to reconstruct what the authors wrote since we don't have the originals. And so you have to reconstruct the originals because you don't have them. That's true for Herodotus, Thucydides, Julius Caesar, Livy, and the New Testament. We have a better chance of reconstructing the writings of the New Testament than of any other book from the ancient world. That's absolutely right, and it's absolutely irrelevant to the question of whether we can trust the Bible on the historical Jesus. Let me give you an illustration of why.

Several years ago I wrote a book titled *Misquoting Jesus*.[48] You will have no trouble reconstructing my original words. As opposed to 5,700 manuscripts that we have of the New Testament, there are 300,000 copies of my book in print, and all 300,000 copies are exactly alike. You can reconstruct what I said with complete accuracy. Does that mean that you can trust what I said? I assure you, the answer is no. Knowing what I wrote is irrelevant to the question of whether you can trust what I wrote. The fact that we have more manuscripts of the New Testament is not relevant to this topic: "Can we trust the Bible on the historical Jesus?"

The next issue that I want to talk about is Craig's second major point, that the Gospels contain numerous verisimilitudes.

---

48. See n. 15 above.

They show that these people know about first-century life. They know people who lived in the first century; they are accurate about customs and laws of the time. My response is "Of course, they are accurate about the times. They *lived* in the times." That is again irrelevant to the question of whether we can trust what they have to say about the historical Jesus, and I'll tell you why.

Suppose that in two thousand years from now, archaeologists discover a newspaper in which it is stated that Duke University played the University of North Carolina, Chapel Hill, in basketball on February 13, 2011. The article states that the University of North Carolina was located in Chapel Hill, North Carolina; that it was twelve miles away from Duke University, which was located in Durham; and that in the game UNC won by a score of 93–75. Go Heels!

There would be considerable verisimilitude in that story. It's true that Duke is located in Durham, North Carolina; that UNC is located in Chapel Hill; that they are twelve miles apart, both have good basketball teams, and played basketball this year. It's absolutely right: the verisimilitude is right up and down the line, and the facts of the story are precisely wrong at every point. The game was not on February 13. UNC did not win the game but lost. And there is injustice in the universe.

Just because a source contains verisimilitude doesn't mean that it can be trusted. We are interested in knowing if what the New Testament says about the historical Jesus is accurate or not. The answer is no. I was especially struck by the fact that Craig agrees with me. He didn't put it as strongly as I did, but he agrees. The New Testament is filled with discrepancies. If you have two accounts of what Jesus did and they contradict each other, they cannot both be historically accurate. They might be interesting. They might be great stories. They might be theologically significant. But they can't be historically accurate if they contradict one another. And the fact is that the Gospels contradict one another up and down the line.

Craig ended his talk by quoting E. P. Sanders, who used to teach, I am sorry to say, at Duke University. (My wife, by the way, teaches at Duke University, and there is a big rivalry, as you may know, between Duke University and the University of North Carolina at Chapel Hill when it comes to basketball. My wife and I got married ten years ago, and we worked out a deal. The deal was that we would live near the Duke Campus if she would root for the Tar Heels. It's a very good deal.)

There are discrepancies, and the discrepancies show that they cannot be accurate. I have not actually given some of the biggest problems; I have focused on little details. There are big problems, and let me just tell you one of the big problems. The Gospel of John portrays Jesus very differently from Matthew, Mark, and Luke. Why? Because it was written much later by somebody who didn't have access to Matthew, Mark, and Luke. In John's Gospel, Jesus says things about himself that he does not say in any of our earlier Gospels. John is being written about sixty years after Jesus died. In John's Gospel, Jesus makes amazing claims about himself. And he does this only in the Gospel of John. Here Jesus says such things as these: "I am the resurrection and the life. I am the light of the world. I am the way, the truth, and the life. No one comes to the Father but by me. I and the Father are one. Before Abraham was, I am." Jesus' opponents knew full well what he was saying; they picked up stones to stone him for claiming that he was equal with God. A human, equal with God? Yes, according to the Gospel of John and only according to the Gospel of John, this is Jesus' claim. That he in some sense is actually divine. That he existed with God before he came into the world. His teaching about himself is that he is equal with God, just as the author of John says at the very beginning of his Gospel: "In the beginning was the word, and the word was with God, and the word was God. Through him all things came into being, and apart from him nothing came into being that came into being. In him was life, and his life was the light of humans. The light shines in the darkness, and the darkness has not overcome it."

In the Gospel of John, Jesus in some sense is equal with God: he calls himself that. So let me ask a simple question: Why do you not find that teaching in Matthew, Mark, and

Luke—the earlier Gospels? Why does Jesus not call himself God in Matthew, Mark, and Luke, the earlier Gospels? If Jesus really went around calling himself God, don't you think somebody would want to report that? Did the other Gospels just forget to mention that part? It's the most important thing. Why isn't it in our earlier Gospels? I believe it's not in the earlier Gospels because Jesus said no such thing about himself. This is the view of the Gospel of John. It may be theologically important, [even] extremely significant theologically, but it's not historically accurate. Thank you very much.

CRAIG EVANS: RESPONSE

Let me make something very clear on the point about the manuscripts. I think that's exactly where historians do begin: they do review the nature of the evidence. They want to see what they have to work with. And I wanted you to know that the Gospels stand up very well, the New Testament writings in general, but the focus is more on the Gospels, as I said. We are talking about the historical Jesus and asking whether we find an accurate portrait of the historical Jesus in the Gospels. As you will recall, I began my comments by saying that indeed we can. So, I do not think that the number and date of the manuscripts is irrelevant. No historian would think that. And if the oldest manuscript we had was five or six hundred years removed from the autograph, if we suspected that the author of the Gospel lived 150 or 200 years after the time of Jesus, that would change things a lot. In fact, that's part of the reason we have difficulties with the *Gospel of Thomas* and the *Gospel of Peter*. I know that some of the popular media and some popular books try to smuggle parts of these writings into the first century; there are attempts to date them as early as possible. Scholars who do that know they need to do that in order to make the case that these apocryphal Gospels come close to rivaling the first-century Gospels, which are canonical. So no, I don't think the number and age of these manuscripts is irrelevant to the question of the historical Jesus, but it's not the only factor. There are other things to consider, such as the question of verisimilitude. Bart gave us an interesting example. If I found a source that was talking about Duke and some rivalry and so on, and Duke was placed in Georgia, I'd have a problem with that, also if Duke was placed in any wrong city or wrong state. Don't tell me that that is unimportant; and again I go back to the comparison. Some of my colleagues in the Jesus Seminar lionize the *Gospel of Thomas*. I find that frustrating because all of the markers in *Thomas* point to the second century, the second half of that century in Syria. There is no historical verisimilitude in *Thomas* as it relates to the first century, the first half of the first century in Jewish Palestine. That is very important. No, it's not the only question because a bunch of uninformed dishonest people from first-century Palestine could make up stories that would betray verisimilitude. I realize that. But that's why there are several factors that come into play. We have multiply attested material. We don't just have the one account that erroneously announces some detail about a basketball game. We have several accounts, and they can be cross-examined. We have sources outside of the Gospels. There were some rather confident positions that scholars took at one time, and the Dead Sea Scrolls embarrassed them.

For example, they said things like this: "Matthew created the reply of Jesus to John the Baptist when John was discouraged in prison, and John sent messengers to Jesus, asking, 'Are you really the one to come, or should we look for somebody else?'" It's funny how Matthew introduces that story; Luke doesn't do it that way. Luke introduces this little anecdote with the words "when John heard about the works of the Messiah." And guess what we find in a scroll: our closest parallel to Jesus' reply, which was, "Go back and tell John what you are seeing here: the blind regain their sight, the dead are being raised up, lepers are cleansed, the poor have good news preached to them." It turns out that a scroll from Cave 4 is talking about things that happen when the Messiah, whom heaven and earth obey, arrives on the scene. Looks like Matthew had it right. That's what I am talking about. Verisimilitude is very important. But let's get back to the discrepancies and the really big problem.

Sure, John is different, but the question is genre. What exactly is John? That's a major question. It's a question that I wrestle with too. Early church fathers wrestled with it as well. They weren't sure if John should be retained and read in the churches because it was so different from Matthew, Mark, and Luke. It is very different, so many Johannine scholars aren't sure Jesus said these kinds of things, these long discourses. Some have suggested that they are third-person statements: *he* is the way and the truth and the life; he is the light of the world; he is the good shepherd. They may be third-person confessions, which in dramatic form are presented then in the first person. So then the question, as Bart said, is a question of theology. And yet John is curiously studded with little historical details and pieces of information that Johannine scholars today are actually talking about in the Society of Biblical Literature program unit that deals with the Gospel of John and the historical Jesus. So this whole thing is being reviewed. But you have to get the genre correct first to know what kind of literature this is. We tend to foist our modern, Western views on documents from antiquity that we don't understand very well. And then when they don't measure up, we have a crisis of confidence and faith.

The Gospels are not photographs; they are not videotapes. No history is a videotape unless it's a videotape in modern times. It is an interpretative portrait; and therefore a historical personage from George Washington to Julius Caesar, or whomever, is a construct. History is not a mirror or a videotape of word for word. Think about it. Think about Peter's Pentecost sermon. How long does it take to read? Two minutes? I guess that's it. He stood up—that was the moment—before a huge audience, and he preached for two minutes. And you know what we learn from that, pastors? You stop that sermon after two minutes, and you will have a very successful altar call. That is a condensation. There could be some word-for-word parts—*ipsissima verba Petrou*. There could be some of the very words that Peter spoke—two or three in a row—but it's a condensation. The

Greeks have a word for it: it's called an epitome, a summary. His sermon in chapter 3 of Acts takes just twenty seconds longer to read. The Sermon on the Mount, the way it's been constructed by Matthew, takes a little longer; it's not just two minutes. It takes longer than that to read. So what? Jesus sits down and teaches and after ten minutes says, "Okay, let's go." Really? We need to understand the genre. I didn't talk much about that earlier, so I am glad that Bart raised these points. It gives me an opportunity to say something about that. We understand the pedagogy; we need to understand how they taught, not as on tape recorders but as thinkers and appliers and adapters. And we need to know what the genre is that has been produced at the end of that process. We need to get out of the rigid thinking. And many of us have lived there and some of us still live there. I don't want to insult anyone and say, "You know, it's a fundamentalist universe," or something like that—so I won't call it that. But it's a rigid, unrealistic, and inaccurate understanding of the genre. And if we can't get that set right, we will continue to spin in circles and say, "Oh dear! I don't know what to do with these discrepancies. They can't both be true." You may as well take two portraits by a great painter and notice the differences in the colors: they can't both be true. That's an erroneous analogy. That's part of the problem. Thank you.

BART EHRMAN: CONCLUSION

Okay, well, thank you again. I have enjoyed very much being with you this evening. I think it's been a very stimulating time; it's been great doing this. I want to point out that Craig and I are agreeing. At the end he may say that we are disagreeing, but we are agreeing. He has just told you that Jesus did not say the things in the Gospel of John that he is quoted as saying. Peter did not give the speech in Acts the way it says in Acts. He says we have to look at the genre. Absolutely right! The genres of these books are not histories. The topic we are to be debating is whether we can trust what the Bible says about the historical Jesus. We are debating whether it's historically accurate, and we both agree that the answer is no because of the genre of these writings.

Let me close by just explaining quickly why these books are historically inaccurate. Jesus died sometime around the year 30 of the Common Era. The Gospels were not written right away. Jesus spoke Aramaic. Stories about him circulated in Palestine in Aramaic, and the stories about Jesus circulated year after year outside of Palestine. The stories circulated as Christians were trying to convert others to the faith. If you wanted somebody to stop being a pagan and to become a follower of Jesus, you had to convince them that Jesus was somebody special, and so you told them stories about Jesus. You told them stories you heard. Where did you hear the stories? Were you there to see the stories happen? Not if you live in Ephesus or in Rome. You heard the stories. Well, from whom did you hear the stories? You heard them from somebody else who heard the stories. Well, where did they hear them from? They heard them from their spouse. Where did their spouse hear them from? They heard them from the next-door neighbor. Where did the next-door neighbor hear them from? One heard them from the spouse. Where did they hear the stories? Well, there was a businessman who came into town and told the stories. Well, where did he hear them from?

These stories are not being told just by apostles. People are becoming Christian throughout the Roman Empire on the basis of stories they have heard about Jesus. The stories are circulating by word of mouth. Not just month after month but also year after year and decade after decade before somebody writes them down.

What happens to stories that circulate orally? They change. If you don't think that your stories change, then try reading the Gospels horizontally. The stories have been changed. The writers of the Gospels have heard the stories. Now the stories have been translated from Aramaic to an entirely different language, Greek. The Gospel authors write down what they heard. They weren't there to see these things happen. These Gospel writers were not among the first twelve disciples; these books are written anonymously by highly educated Greek-speaking Christians. They were not lower-class peasants who spoke Aramaic in Palestine; they were written by Greek Christians who have heard the stories that have been changed year after year, and they themselves changed the stories. If you don't think they changed the stories, read them horizontally. The stories got changed in the process of transmission, and they were changed again when they were written down.

Let me emphasize this: I am not saying that you should become an agnostic and throw out your Bibles. I am not saying that you should be an unbeliever. I am not saying that you should decide that the Bible is of no use to you. If you accept the Bible, you should accept it for what it is: a document of faith that is not a history book. It is not historically accurate. It is filled with discrepancies. It is filled with stories that didn't happen. There was no census under Caesar Augustus that required everybody to go to their ancestral home from 1,000 years earlier. It didn't happen. It's a story. It's not history. Discrepancies. Contradictions. Implausibilities. Why? Because these Gospels were not written for twenty-first-century people who wanted to do research into first-century Palestine. They were books intended to declare and proclaim the good news of Jesus. That's why they are Gospels. They are not histories. Thank you very much.

CRAIG EVANS: CONCLUSION

Thank you again, Bart. And thank you too for being sufficiently disagreeable on this occasion. No, the Gospels are not histories in a modern sense. In this case we can say, neither is Thucydides, neither is Tacitus; in fact, nobody is in antiquity. Consider the question before us: *Are the New Testament Gospels sufficient for a historian to extract data from them or construct a portrait?* Of course, we can't make our title for the Greer-Heard Conference today that long, so it asks, "Can we trust the

Bible on the historical Jesus?" That's a little clumsy, but what it's asking is clarified in the longer question [above]—at least this is the way I interpret it; if I am wrong, Bob Stewart can straighten me out. You need to understand that scholars make these kinds of distinctions. You can't go on a time machine and fly back two thousand years and videotape Jesus. You can't access Julius Caesar or Alexander the Great, but you can look at the traces, the documents, the sources and from them construct a modern historical portrait. Can we do that? Can we do that fairly, not with everyone agreeing on each point, but can we do that with the Gospels—at least with Matthew, Mark, and Luke because there is still that genre question with John? You know what? A lot of New Testament interpreters think so. A lot of them. There are lots of books, and some of them are rather good and some of them aren't. But it's an industry; there is a historical-Jesus section often attended by two or three hundred people at the annual SBL meeting. That's a funny SBL section to have if it's impossible and just can't be done. So I just want to challenge that and also that thing about stories. Bart sometimes has called it a telephone game, but it didn't work like that. Yes, there were people telling stories and stories, but those aren't the stories that ultimately wound up in the Gospels by the people who did the teaching. So yes, some Christian could hear something and pass on stories. Indeed, they did. Some of the second- and third-century infancy Gospels and other things show what kinds of stories can be told. But I do correct one thing I did not say in reference to Acts 2 and the Pentecost sermon (here I wrote down Bart's words), "Peter didn't say what it says." That's not what I said. I am saying it's not a word-for-word videotape recording of what he said, but an epitome, a summary. I have students come up to me after a one-hour lecture and say, "Professor, help me now. Did I understand you right? Did you say . . . ?" And they give me about a four- or five-second summary of my lecture, and sometimes my response is "Exactly; you got it just right." I didn't really say that at all, but it was a correct summary. I'd be perfectly pleased for someone to write it down and say, "This is what Professor Evans taught in that class." And sometimes they don't have it right. Then I say, "What? Did I say that? I must have misspoken." So I want to be clear on that: this is not a little game here. It's a very important thing. Scholars do talk about this whole question of genre, and this is part of the struggle we have in exegesis and in hermeneutics and in all of these fancy things. And that is because there is a wide gap between us and that period of time two thousand years ago that we so treasure and want to study. So, what we have are portraits, and we can extract from these early sources what I think is an accurate and reasonable picture, incomplete to be sure, and in places uncertain, with discrepancies that frustrate us as modern historians. We wish we knew which it was. Did this happen on Saturday, or did this happen on Friday? We don't know. One Gospel writer presents it this way because that's what he thinks it is. I acknowledge that. Those discrepancies are there. But do we find in these Gospels portraits of the historical Jesus? So, in the words of Ed Sanders, "Do we know what Jesus was talking about and what he was doing?" And I think the answer for that is, "Yes, we do!" Thank you.

Questions and Answers

Let's have some questions. One thing we strive for in a Greer-Heard Conference is to provide a level playing field. So, if you think that you agree more with Bart Ehrman, come to this microphone, and if you think that you agree more with Craig Evans, go to that microphone. We will alternate between the microphones so that we will have balanced input on the questions. So, come to the microphones if you have any questions.

QUESTION 1. This question is for Dr. Evans. You seem to agree at least somewhat about there being at least a few small things that are wrong with the Gospels. So my question is, if it's at least plausible that that's what the evidence suggests, then wouldn't it also be plausible that they got the extraordinary and highly unbelievable things wrong as well, since they were normal human beings writing the Gospels?

EVANS. Anything is possible, but I find your choice of words interesting, "things that are wrong." As I said, interpreters often revel over the differences, so in a sense, we can ask, "What's wrong?" But unless you are saying, "I expect the Gospels to be photographs and videotape and something is wrong," there really isn't a problem. However, if we have two videotapes of an event, and we notice a discrepancy in sequences, that would be strange. That would tell us that something is wrong, because that didn't happen on the videotape. But that's not what the Gospels are; that was the point I was trying to make. And so there are deliberate editorial changes made. Folks, if you do not know that, then do what Professor Ehrman was urging you to do—I urge my students to do that, too—look at the Gospels. If you can read them in Greek, that's even better, but look at them even in English and read them horizontally. He is not making that up: those differences are there. Bart has read the Gospels. They are there. It's what we make of them and if we come to them with—and I am not saying that this is Bart's mind-set—but if we come to the Gospels with the wrong idea of what they're supposed to be, then the discrepancies can be very unsettling. I am aware of that book that Professor Ehrman referred to, *Life of Christ in Stereo*.[1] That is a silly attempt to harmonize the discrepancies, and it shows that something is really wrong with that approach.

Now, what about the plausibility of something really being wrong? This is the issue. For instance, what if it wasn't Jesus who died on the cross and instead it was Simon? There actually were groups in the second century that said Jesus did a bait and switch with Simon of Cyrene. I find that extremely unlikely. I guess you would have to tell me what your big things are that may be wrong: Jesus didn't live, he didn't do something, he never taught any of this, or something else like that? That would be rather implausible. Again, we get back to where I concluded a few minutes ago; if it was that wrong, there wouldn't be too many scholars engaged in this discipline. Thank you for this question.

QUESTION 2. Dr. Ehrman, I find you to be a well-reasoned person who seems to really care about what the Bible says. But

---

1. Cheney, *Life of Christ* (see n. 2 in the "Dialogue" chapter).

whenever I come across people who have a problem with the historicity of Jesus, I always run into what seems like the same problem. And it seems to be something like you've been saying tonight. It doesn't matter that there are numerous early documents, more so than any other ancient text in history. It doesn't matter that there are details in the text indicating that there were eyewitnesses. It doesn't matter that there is archaeological evidence. Where there are differences, they say that the Bible is wrong. And my question is this: If the Bible and the account of Jesus can't be trusted, what does this account look like if it doesn't look like the truth? What would you need historically to be convinced?

EHRMAN. What do historians look for in historical sources if they think they are historical sources? That's a very good question. What do historians want when dealing with a person in the past—it doesn't matter if it is Jesus, or if it's Napoleon, or if it's Julius Caesar, anyone—what do you want? These are the kinds of sources you want: You want lots of sources. You want sources that are close to the time when the event transpired. You want the sources to basically tell the same story without contradicting each other. You want them to be consistent, and yet you don't want them to have collaborated with each other because otherwise one of them will have gotten the story from the other. So that's what you really want. Now, with the Gospels, you have good news and bad news. You get more than one source, so that's good. They are not particularly close to the event. Craig is right: they are closer to the events than other historical sources, but that's kind of below standard, because most historical sources are 100 years later, so they are no good at all. So these are better: they are 30–40 years later, but it's 30–40 years later that you first get the accounts. And they do have discrepancies with one another, and of course they have collaborated. Craig and I are agreeing on this. I agree that you can find the historical Jesus using sources, but that doesn't make the sources historically accurate. The reason historians have to dig to find historically accurate information is because the Gospels themselves are not historically accurate. If the Gospels were historically accurate, we would not have to do scholarship. All you would have to do is read the New Testament and say, "That's what Jesus said and did." There'd be no scholarship involved at all. The fact that there is scholarship and that people like Craig edit books like *Authenticating the Words of Jesus*[2]—he also edited another book called *Authenticating the Activities of Jesus*[3]—the reason he had to prepare those books is precisely because the Gospels don't tell it like it was. If they did, there would be no need for scholarship. Thank you. That's a very good question.

QUESTION 3. Dr. Evans, I have a question for you. For a believer who has gone to church and private schools his whole life, and had religion classes and so on, and was taught that every word of the Bible is true, that it is the infallible Word of God, what would be your response to someone who says, "Bart has proved that there is contradiction and error"? The question is not about walking away from God. But what would you say to the person who says that?

EVANS. Well, we come back to the question of genre and the distinction between history and truth: so is this a true statement, and are we talking about history? For example, Jesus' greatest truths are conveyed as parables, made-up stories. In other words, they are fictional stories, not historical events. By the way, some conservatives are so concerned about that: I have actually heard people try to argue that the parables aren't made-up stories. They say that these are things Jesus saw and experienced, that he's reporting. I've even had people ask, "How did Jesus observe the Good Samaritan and the man who was mugged on the road and left for dead?" They say Jesus saw it because it was Jesus himself who was mugged on the road.

---

2. Bruce Chilton and Craig A. Evans, eds., *Authenticating the Words of Jesus*, NTTS 28.1 (Boston: Brill, 2002).
3. Bruce Chilton and Craig A. Evans, eds., *Authenticating the Activities of Jesus*, NTTS 28.2 (Boston: Brill, 2002).

There is, of course, no reason to think this, but some people are driven to this view because of their understanding of history and truth. In this case, the parable isn't true unless it happened, that is, unless it is history. But this is mistaken; truth need not be restricted to history. Truth can be conveyed through almost any kind of genre: a proverb, a parable, a prophetic statement, a pronouncement statement, a didactic instruction, a teaching, or anything else. History, and we are considering it more from a modern point of view, forces us to sift through the material because what we are looking at contains what we would regard as historical in the sense of giving us facts. But other material gives us interpretations and applications that might not provide facts of history but may well provide important truths. It is not always easy to distinguish between what is historical and what is not. That's why we have to do this work. Professor Ehrman is correct at this point. Because of this complexity, we have specialists and scholars who work for years and years and study a whole variety of languages and materials that relate to it. It is challenging.

QUESTION 4. Dr. Ehrman, if I understood you correctly, you said that we can't trust the New Testament documents because they do not stand up to modern standards of historicity, what we consider with our modern sensibilities to be historically accurate. If in one hundred years, say, the standards for historical accuracy change, would that then mean that we should throw out every document that we currently consider historically accurate? Does everything have to match up to what is at the moment considered accurate?

EHRMAN. Good question. Do you have another question? [Laughter.] No, it's a good question. I think all of us are creatures of our time. I suppose that we are asking ourselves, "Can we trust the Bible to give us historically accurate information?" If so, I think that all we can do is apply what we now know. We don't know what people are going to know in a hundred years. In direct answer to your question, I think the answer is absolutely yes. There are documents today that we may trust as historically accurate, yet in a hundred years people are going to realize they are not accurate. And when that happens, then we won't trust them anymore. People used to trust the Bible as historically accurate, and many people still do, but I think scholarship still shows that we can't trust these books as historical sources—as modern people who have certain expectations of history. Ancient people didn't have the same expectations of history that we have today. So these books might have been perfectly fine as historical sources in the first century, but first-century people would not have asked the question "Can we trust them historically?" That is not the question they would have asked. That's a modern question. And the answer to that modern question is no because they don't live up to our standards of what is required of historical sources. Thank you, though.

QUESTION 5. I have a question for Dr. Evans. What is more important to believers today, the historical data concerning Jesus or the standard of how he taught us to live?

EVANS. That's a good question. And to a certain extent, as far as I am concerned, you can't completely separate them. What Jesus did, the things he really said, a fair and accurate summary of his teachings, and the kinds of things he did—all these are closely connected. Some of the task is exegetical as well, to understand what he in fact demanded of those who would follow him. But at the end of the day I would say, if you really well understand the historical Jesus and what he taught, and you don't do it, such study is pointless. So what counts is putting into practice what Jesus taught and required of his disciples. Very thoughtful question. Thank you.

QUESTION 6. Professor Ehrman, you stated that we should be able to take the theological content of the Scriptures in the New Testament as instructive while not necessarily trusting the historical information. My question is this: how can we trust theological judgments that were based on these supposed historical events that the authors came to base their theological conclusions on?

EHRMAN. Yes, thank you. My view is that these sources were not intending to present what we think of as historically accurate information; that's a modern imposition on these Gospels that they can't bear. And so they weren't basing theological judgments on what they thought were historically accurate pieces of information. They were trying to tell what they understood to be truth claims about Jesus. My view is that you need to judge those truth claims independently of whether or not what they say about Jesus is historically accurate or not. I am not championing these truth claims. I am not saying that we should believe these truth claims. But I am saying that their evaluation should be independent of whether or not they are historical because these people did not have our sense of historical accuracy.

QUESTION 7. It's for Professor Ehrman. I just had a question really of historical inaccuracy. It seems to me, in the Gospels and in Josephus, we see the Jews time and again, Jewish authorities, stoning people to death, not the least of which are killed or killing people, not the least of which are John the Baptist or Stephen. So why, at the point of Jesus' death, is it now not possible for the Jews to put somebody to death, and it has to be done by Romans? I have always seen that as kind of a historical inconsistency within the Gospels themselves.

EHRMAN. Yeah, thank you. That's an interesting question. There are debates among Roman historians about what was permitted by ruling authorities in the provinces. Judea was ruled as a Roman province. It was governed by a Roman governor, by administrators. The local authority was the Jewish Sanhedrin, which was the local Jewish council that consisted of the aristocrats with the leaders of the Jews, but they had to report to the Roman authorities because the Romans had authority over Judea. And it appears that one of the things that local authorities were not allowed to do was to execute criminals. This was something that was reserved for the authorities; the Romans retained the right of capital punishment to themselves. There are incidents, of course, in which you have something like mob violence. So the account of Stephen being stoned is not an account of an official juridical process: it's an account of mob violence. So that would be different from Jesus, who is put up for crimes against the state. It's very important to emphasize that it was historically—I think Craig and I absolutely agree on this as well—it was the Romans who killed Jesus. And over the centuries, of course, it came to be thought that the Jews killed Jesus. Well, the Jews did not kill Jesus: the Romans killed Jesus. Of course, not all Romans did: Pontius Pilate ordered it. So it's important to keep that straight. One of the things that's interesting, by the way, is that over the course of time, when Christians described Pilate's role in the death of Jesus, Pilate was portrayed as increasingly innocent over time in the various Gospels; through the New Testament Gospels and then into the second century. The Christians started to portray Pilate as increasingly innocent because of this reason: if he is innocent, who is guilty? The Jews. So that's how Jews come to be thought of as at fault, but historically, of course, it was Pilate himself, and it's for this reason that the Romans reserved the right of capital punishment to themselves.

QUESTION 8. Dr. Ehrman, in your illustration of the four Jimmy Carter biographies, the four biographers in the scenario have never met Jimmy Carter. Is it your perspective that none of the four canonical Gospels was written by eyewitnesses? If they were not themselves eyewitnesses, were they in contact with eyewitnesses? If you do not believe so, what is your opinion of the work of Richard Bauckham's book *Jesus and the Eyewitnesses*?[4]

EHRMAN. Right. My view is that none of the Gospel writers was an eyewitness. None of them claims to be an eyewitness. If you read the Gospel of Matthew, the author never says, "My

---

4. Richard Bauckham, *Jesus and the Eyewitnesses: The Gospels as Eyewitness Testimony* (Grand Rapids: Eerdmans, 2006).

name is Matthew." He never narrates anything in the first person. He never says, "Jesus and I went to Jerusalem." He never says, "This is what I and the other disciples did." When Matthew describes the call of Matthew to be a disciple, he describes it in the third person about something happening to someone else. It's written in the third person by an author who does not claim to be an eyewitness. Later editors put a title on it, "The Gospel according to Matthew." But that isn't who was writing it. If Matthew wrote a Gospel, he wouldn't title it "The Gospel according to Matthew." Right. That's somebody telling you who wrote this particular Gospel at a later time. There was a later tradition that the Gospel of Matthew was written by Matthew the disciple, but the Gospel itself doesn't claim so, and I think the answer to the question is "Absolutely not." Matthew the disciple did not write the Gospel of Matthew. Whoever wrote Matthew was a highly educated Greek-speaking person who lived outside of Palestine, who was probably living, I would say, 50–55 years—this is a common date, I think Craig probably agrees with this—50 or 55 years after the death of Jesus. I don't think he was an eyewitness, and I don't think he had access to eyewitnesses. I find Richard Bauckham's book to be absolutely unpersuasive.

QUESTION 9. Thank you. My question is for both speakers. If we don't trust the historical accuracy of the Bible, it goes to the interaction between the theological Bible and the historical Bible; if the Bible really is, as Dr. Evans says, a living and adaptable tradition and if it's not historically accurate, what does someone do who is struggling to decide what they believe about the tenets of the New Testament regarding sin? Where do we go next?

EVANS. What I am trying to say is that it is important to recognize the genre of the biblical literature—each book, each passage. Only when we correctly identify the genre are we in a position to recognize what is making a claim to history. Sometimes things that aren't claiming to be history may in fact give away some important information and hints about the time and place in which it was written. So, I wouldn't frame the question the way you did. It's a question of the study of each book that's in the Bible and its components and pieces to understand exactly what it is. Now, there are naive readers who think that the whole Bible is history. Or they make the equation: if this isn't history, then it's not true. I have actually had students who say that, to go back to what I said about parables, as I remarked earlier. When I say these are stories that are made up, a little fictional story about somebody who was on the road to Jericho, or a sower, or a farmer who pitched seed on the ground, I have actually had students come and ask, "Do you mean they are not true?" That is, if the parable isn't actual history, then it cannot be true. This, of course, is false. So we need to work really hard so that we can get that sorted out. There are religious writings and other traditions in which there is no history at all, but there are adherents who say, "This is the truth, and I live by it." So it's very important that we make that distinction.

EHRMAN. I'll be very quick. I completely agree with Craig on this point.

The State of the Quest for the Historical Jesus

ROBERT B. STEWART

Of scholarly research on the historical Jesus, there seems to be no end. Yet when I was a seminary student in the late 1980s, it was not uncommon to hear that the quest for the historical Jesus had come to an end and that it was largely a failure. This opinion was a result of Albert Schweitzer's monumental 1906 book, *The Quest of the Historical Jesus*,[1] in which he critiqued life-of-Jesus research up to his day. Schweitzer's book was a keen and insightful analysis of the scholarly work concerning Jesus from Reimarus to Wrede, but more importantly, it was a rhetorical tour de force; Schweitzer's style was captivating and even shocking at points.

The broad outlines of the history of historical-Jesus research are well known to students and scholars in the field. The names Reimarus, Paulus, Strauss, Renan, Holtzmann, Ritschl, Harnack, Kähler, Wrede, Schweitzer, Bultmann, Käsemann, Bornkamm, and Robinson have been repeated many times. The sketch is so well known that undergraduate students can

---

1. Albert Schweitzer, *The Quest of the Historical Jesus: A Critical Study of Its Progress from Reimarus to Wrede*, trans. W. Montgomery (New York: Macmillan, 1968).

easily cram into their minds the outline of First Quest, No Quest, New Quest, and Third Quest, although they may not be able to supply much more in the way of understanding. Of course this outline is simplistic and distorting,[2] but it is also useful as a heuristic device. The philosophical and cultural influences—such as enlightenment rationality, deism, Spinoza's biblical criticism, Kant's separation of the noumenal from the phenomenal, Hegel's historical dialectic, Lessing's skepticism, and Liberal moralism—are less obvious but still there for those with eyes to see.

Many wrongly believe that Schweitzer intended to bring the Quest to its end; he did not. Instead, he concluded that previous Quests had failed because they tried to force Jesus into the mold of a modern man. That left only two options for Jesus research in the future: Schweitzer's model of thoroughgoing eschatology or Wrede's model of thoroughgoing skepticism. For the most part Schweitzer's words have proved to be prophetic. For the greater part of the twentieth century, skepticism as modeled in form-and-redaction criticism prevailed; but in the late twentieth century, eschatology and a tempered historical optimism made a comeback in the Third Quest.

The last forty years have seen some quite exciting work take place in the field of historical-Jesus studies. Paradigm-challenging works have come from E. P. Sanders,[3] John Dominic Crossan,[4] N. T. Wright,[5] and James D. G. Dunn.[6] Additionally, the volumes in John P. Meier's *Marginal Jew* series are both massively detailed and massively informed.[7] It is no

---

2. On the distorting power of this now standard outline, see F. Bermejo Rubio, "The Fiction of the 'Three Quests': An Argument for Dismantling a Dubious Historiographical Paradigm," *JSHJ* 7 (2009): 211–53. See also Stanley E. Porter, *The Criteria of Authenticity in Historical-Jesus Research: Previous Discussion and New Proposals*, JSNTSup 191 (Sheffield: Sheffield Academic Press, 2000), 28–62.

3. E. P. Sanders, *Jesus and Judaism* (Philadelphia: Fortress Press, 1985).

4. John Dominic Crossan, *Historical Jesus: The Life of a Mediterranean Jewish Peasant* (San Francisco: Harper & Row, 1991).

5. N. T. Wright, *Jesus and the Victory of God*, vol. 2 of *Christian Origins and the Question of God* (Minneapolis: Fortress Press, 1996).

6. James D. G. Dunn, *Jesus Remembered*, vol. 1 of *Christianity in the Making* (Grand Rapids: Wm. B. Eerdmans Publishing Co., 2003.

7. John P. Meier, *A Marginal Jew: Rethinking the Historical Jesus*, 5 vols., ABRL (New York: Doubleday, 1991–2016).

exaggeration to say that the past forty years have been the most productive in the history of the Quest.

Overshadowed by these larger and more spectacular projects, a great deal of progress has also been made through methodological studies, monographs, anthologies, and journal articles. One could even argue that the most significant work has taken place in the relative shadows. One word sums up this often-overlooked work: *reevaluation*. Here I briefly touch on four areas that, in my estimation, are significant in that they have the potential to overthrow the status quo of Jesus research.

MEMORY STUDIES

One of the more interesting and hotly contested areas of recent Jesus research has been that of memory. In *Jesus Remembered*, James D. G. Dunn argues that the only Jesus available to historians is the remembered Jesus: the impression that Jesus made upon his earliest followers. Significantly, Dunn insists that these memories were pre-Easter memories and that there was a significant continuity between the earliest memories of Jesus and the written Gospels. Another major work challenging skeptical post-Bultmannian theories is Richard Bauckham's *Jesus and the Eyewitnesses*.[8] Anthony Le Donne's 2009 book, *The Historiographical Jesus*,[9] agrees that the only Jesus available to historians is the remembered Jesus, but he also insists that the remembered Jesus is the *interpreted* Jesus. In my opinion, all three of these books challenge the standard view that hypothesizes an evolutionary oral period leading to layers of literary development by appealing to the memory of eyewitnesses.

But is memory reliable? This is a reasonable question. Judith C. S. Redman thinks it is not. She cites psychological research on eyewitness memory, research indicating that several factors can

---

8. Bauckham, *Jesus and the Eyewitnesses*.
9. Anthony Le Donne, *The Historiographical Jesus: Memory, Typology, and the Son of David* (Waco, TX: Baylor University Press, 2009).

inhibit accuracy, such as a desire to agree with other witnesses, guessing about elements of their reports, and the hardening of false memories.[10] Redman writes, "The continued presence in Christian communities of eyewitnesses to Jesus' ministry until the time when these events were recorded is a guarantee only of the community's agreed version, not of the exact details of the event itself."[11]

To some extent Robert McIver agrees with Redman. His findings say that roughly 80 percent of what eyewitnesses report can be verified, but in various writings[12] he also points out that even their false memories are consistent with their true memories. In other words, they retain the gist of the event. Suffice it to say that there is more to be said on this important topic.

DATING THE GOSPELS

The most significant voice arguing for an early date to the Synoptic Gospels is secular scholar James G. Crossley. He accepts Markan priority but argues that rather than being written in the late 60s or early 70s, Mark could have been written as early as the mid-30s.[13] Crossley is hardly the first to argue for an early date. In 1976 John A. T. Robinson argued that the majority date was mistaken: "One of the oddest facts about the New Testament is that what on any showing would appear to be the single most datable and climactic event of the period—the fall of Jerusalem in AD 70, and with it the collapse of institutional Judaism based on the temple—is never once mentioned as a past fact."[14]

---

10. Judith C. S. Redman, "How Accurate Are Eyewitnesses? Bauckham and the Eyewitnesses in the Light of Psychological Research," *JBL* 129 (2010): 177–93.

11. Redman, "How Accurate Are Eyewitnesses?," 193.

12. Robert K. McIver, *Memory, Jesus, and the Synoptic Gospels*, SBLRBS (Atlanta: Society of Biblical Literature, 2011), esp. 60–70; McIver, "Eyewitnesses as Guarantors of the Accuracy of the Gospel Traditions in the Light of Psychological Research," *JBL* 131 (2012): 530–33; and McIver, "Collective Memory and the Reliability of the Gospel Traditions," in *Jesus, Skepticism, and the Problem of History: Criteria and Context in the Study of Christian Origins*, ed. Darrell L. Bock and J. Ed Komoszewski (Grand Rapids: Zondervan, 2019), 125–44.

13. James G. Crossley, *The Date of Mark's Gospel* (London: T&T Clark International, 2004), 22–24.

14. John A. T. Robinson, *Redating the New Testament* (London: SCM Press, 1976), 13.

Even earlier and via multiple points, Adolf von Harnack had argued for an earlier dating of the Gospels. Harnack agreed with most source critics that Mark was the first Gospel but for many reasons also insisted that Mark was written significantly earlier than most scholars then—or now—think. One reason was that Acts does not mention the result of Paul's trial, which Harnack regarded as an appalling lacuna.[15] Another reason supporting his first argument is that nowhere in Acts does the reader find any instance of the death of Peter or Paul presupposed, or even prophesied, though many other events are prophesied.[16] Harnack also notes that nothing is said of Nero's persecution of Christians or the events of the First Jewish-Roman War (AD 66–73). Yet these are all arguments from silence; in a formal sense they do not prove that the majority position is incorrect. Nevertheless, historical theories are never proved in such a way; the conjunction of several significant absences should attract the historian's attention.

Crossley mentions these earlier arguments from Harnack and Robinson, but his argument for redating Mark goes beyond them and is more sophisticated in that it is based on exegesis of what the text actually says and on consideration of the different ways in which Mark, Matthew, and Luke treat issues of biblical law versus the expanded (oral) law of the scribes and Pharisees. He insists that the Synoptic Gospels never picture Jesus as breaking a biblical law and gives close attention to passages dealing with the Sabbath (Mark 2:23–28; Matt. 12:1–8; Luke 6:1–5) and with divorce and remarriage (Mark 10:1–12; Matt. 19:1–9).[17] Yet within two decades of Jesus' death, Christians were discarding these laws. Crossley infers that Mark reflects a cultural milieu in which Christians observed the biblical law prior to a significant influx of Gentile

---

15. Adolf von Harnack, *The Date of the Acts and the Synoptic Gospels*, trans. J. R. Wilkinson, vol. 4 of *New Testament Studies* (New York: G. P. Putnam's Sons, 1911), 96–97, esp. 97: "Throughout eight whole chapters St Luke keeps his readers intensely interested in the progress of the trial of St Paul, simply that he may in the end completely disappoint them—they learn nothing of the final result of the trial! . . . If St Luke, in the year 80, 90, or 100, wrote thus he was not simply a blundering but an absolutely incomprehensible historian!"
16. Harnack, *Date of the Acts and the Synoptic Gospels*, 97, 99.
17. Crossley, *Date of Mark's Gospel*, 159–82.

believers and then concludes that Mark was probably written sometime between the late 30s and mid-40s.[18] If Crossley is correct, the direct implication is that the historical Jesus was a faithful Jew who took part in some of the intra-Jewish debates of the first century; the indirect implication is that the standard form-critical view—that the tradition concerning Jesus evolved significantly between Jesus and the Synoptic Gospels—is seriously weakened.

The strongest internal argument for the standard view that Mark was written around 70 CE is Mark 13. Crossley discusses this passage at length and concludes that, on the basis of Mark 13 alone, Mark could have been written anywhere "between the mid to late thirties and c. 70."[19] The consensus view may or may not be correct. One cannot argue that Crossley's positions are based on theological reasons (nor can one say that of Harnack or Robinson). One thing appears to be clear: there is more work to be done on this issue.

REASSESSING THE CRITERIA

In 2012, Chris Keith and Anthony Le Donne assembled a stellar ensemble of scholars to challenge those who would employ the standard criteria of authenticity. The result, *Jesus, Criteria, and the Demise of Authenticity*,[20] was a methodological shot across the bow of the consensus critical study of Jesus. Taking their cue from Morna Hooker—whose critical essays were paradigm-challenging compositions,[21] even if few recognized it at the time—their authors forthrightly call for change. Some, like Chris Keith and Scot McKnight, argue for doing away with the criteria approach altogether, albeit for different reasons. Others, like Dagmar Winter, aim not to throw out the baby with the

---

18. Crossley, *Date of Mark's Gospel*, 206–9.
19. Crossley, *Date of Mark's Gospel*, 43.
20. Chris Keith and Anthony Le Donne, eds., *Jesus, Criteria, and the Demise of Authenticity* (New York: T&T Clark, 2012).
21. Morna D. Hooker, "On Using the Wrong Tool," *Theology* 75 (1972): 570–81; Hooker, "Christology and Methodology," *New Testament Studies* 17 (1970–71): 480–87.

bathwater but to replace the existing criteria with newer criteria that more effectively do what the standard methods were intended to do in the first place: identify not only what was distinctive about the historical Jesus but also what was dominant.[22] In addition to the essays in *Jesus, Criteria, and the Demise of Authenticity*, if one is looking for a monograph on the subject, Stanley Porter's *The Criteria for Authenticity in Historical-Jesus Research: Previous Discussion and New Proposals* highlights how those who created the criteria have been misunderstood and how the criteria themselves have been abused; Porter gives some helpful suggestions for how to remedy the situation.[23]

ORAL TRADITION

Prior to the pioneering work of Rudolf Bultmann, Martin Dibelius, and Karl Ludwig Schmidt, critical scholarship of the New Testament was confined largely to text and source criticism.[24] Believing that the oral period between Jesus and the composition of the Gospels was both a matter of decades and a time in which the stories underwent significant alterations to meet the needs of the individual believing communities, they developed form criticism (*Formgeschichte*) to reach back to the oral stage before the written sources. One reason they assumed that the period of oral transmission of the Jesus tradition was largely *evolutionary* in nature was that they compared the different sorts of literature of which the Gospels were composed with the genre of folk literature.[25]

---

22. Chris Keith, "The Fall of the Quest for an Authentic Jesus: Concluding Remarks," in Keith and Le Donne, *Jesus, Criteria*, 200-205; Scot McKnight, "Why the Authentic Jesus Is of No Use for the Church," in Keith and Le Donne, *Jesus, Criteria*, 173-85; Dagmar Winter, "Saving the Quest for Authenticity from the Criterion of Dissimilarity: History and Plausibility," in Keith and Le Donne, *Jesus, Criteria*, 115–31.

23. Porter, *Criteria of Authenticity*.

24. Rudolf Bultmann, *The History of the Synoptic Tradition*, 2nd ed., trans. John Marsh (Oxford: Blackwell, 1968); Martin Dibelius, *From Tradition to Gospel*, trans. Bertram Lee Woolf (London: Nicholson & Watson, 1934); Karl Ludwig Schmidt, *Der Rahman der Geschichte Jesu* (Berlin: Trowitzsch & Sohn, 1919).

25. Dibelius, *From Tradition to Gospel*, 1–4. Bultmann references, among others, the work of the brothers Grimm and Wilhelm Wisser, who were writing in Germany in the 19th century. For example, see Bultmann, *History of the Synoptic Tradition*, 46, 184.

Quite apart from biblical studies, significant work has been done in the past forty years on the nature of oral communities and how they pass on their traditions.[26] These advances have challenged the presuppositions of form critics.

Probably the most significant and easily grasped work has been that of missionary-scholar Kenneth Bailey. Bailey, building on the work of W. D. Davies[27] and C. H. Dodd,[28] along with over thirty years of personal experience while living with and observing oral cultures in the Middle East, suggests that scholars seeking to understand the nature of the earliest oral Jesus stories work within the categories of informal/formal and controlled/uncontrolled oral tradition.[29]

An *informal tradition* is one in which there is no identifiable teacher or student; anyone in the community can tell the story, and there is no identifiable message that is passed on. A *formal tradition* is one with a clearly identified teacher, a clearly identified student, and clearly identified material that is being passed on.

An *uncontrolled tradition* is one where there is no community structure to control or limit what is passed on (how the story is told and thus what the story is). A *controlled tradition* is one where the community has a structure in place to control or limit changes to the message or material that is passed on. The teachers (or teacher) are the primary means of controlling the tradition. Yet the community as a whole can also work to preserve the tradition.

Bailey holds that the category of *informal yet controlled oral tradition* best fits the phenomena found in the Synoptic

---

26. For a helpful survey of the state of contemporary research on oral tradition, see Paul Rhodes Eddy, "The Historicity of the Early Oral Jesus Tradition," in Bock and Komoszewski, *Jesus, Skepticism*, 145–63. See also Jan Vansina, *Oral Tradition as History* (Madison: University of Wisconsin Press, 1985); Ruth Finnegan, *The Oral and Beyond: Doing Things with Words in Africa* (Chicago: University of Chicago Press, 2007); Finnegan, "A Note on Oral Tradition and Historical Evidence," *HistTh* 9 (1970): 195–201; Finnegan, *Literacy and Orality: Studies in the Technology of Communication* (Oxford and New York: Blackwell, 1988), 108–9; Finnegan, *Oral Poetry: Its Nature, Significance and Social Context* (Cambridge: Cambridge University Press, 1977).
27. W. D. Davies, *The Setting of the Sermon on the Mount* (Cambridge: Cambridge University Press, 1964), esp. 466, n. 1; 477.
28. C. H. Dodd, *The Founder of Christianity* (London: Macmillan, 1970), 22.
29. Kenneth E. Bailey, "Informal Controlled Oral Tradition and the Synoptic Gospels," *AsJT* 5, no. 1 (April 1991): 34–54.

Gospels. In such a culture any established member of the community can tell the story (thus informal), but the community controls the degree of variation that is allowed (thus exercising control) through honor-and-shame practices. Additionally, Bailey identifies another way the tradition is controlled: through the presence of eyewitnesses.[30] This fits well with the introduction to Luke.

Significantly, Bailey maintains that material like that found in the Gospels would almost certainly be the sort of oral tradition that a Middle Eastern community would control because this material was essential to the community for its identity. "In the light of the reality described above[,] the assumption that the early Christians were not interested in history becomes untenable. To remember the words and deeds of Jesus of Nazareth was to affirm their own unique identity. The stories had to be *told* and *controlled*[,] or everything that made them who they were was lost."[31]

If Bailey is correct, then the oral culture out of which the written Gospels came was one in which the gist of the story remained stable, although there may have been some changes in minor details. This is what historical reliability would have meant in the first generation of the Christian church.

Opinions differ on Bailey's work. Theodore Weeden presents a skeptical assessment of his work; Dunn is generally optimistic about it.[32] Much of Bailey's work is expressed through anecdotes. He analyzed twentieth-century Middle Eastern oral cultures, not first-century Jewish oral cultures. Yet these Middle Eastern twentieth-century communities were culturally closer to the early church than the Germanic folk tales from which Bultmann and Dibelius drew their conclusions about the nature of the oral tradition. We must also remember that Christianity was birthed in a world that was *primarily* oral, not

---

30. Bailey, "Oral Tradition," 50. This fits somewhat well with Bauckham's thesis in *Jesus and the Eyewitnesses*. Note that Bauckham's model is a formal controlled oral tradition rather than Bailey's informal controlled oral tradition.
31. Bailey, "Oral Tradition," 50–51.
32. Theodore Weeden Sr., "Kenneth Bailey's Theory of Oral Tradition: A Theory Contested by Its Evidence," *JSHJ* 7, no. 1 (2009): 3–43; James D. G. Dunn, "Kenneth Bailey's Theory of Oral Tradition: Critiquing Theodore Weeden's Critique," *JSHJ* 7, no. 1 (January 2009): 44–62.

exclusively oral. One must be careful when drawing conclusions about primarily oral cultures from exclusively oral cultures. One thing is certain: oral cultures are much more sophisticated than scholars in early twentieth-century Europe knew.

As I've stated earlier, these four areas have the potential to change how Jesus research is conducted. But I am unable at this time to know whether the work I've referenced will in fact significantly change any aspect of the study of the historical Jesus. In fact, I expect that at least one of these areas will not have the impact on Jesus studies that I think it has the potential to have. My primary intention, therefore, in including them has been to highlight the fact that historical conclusions inevitably change either due to new evidence coming forward that calls for reevaluation or because historians, being properly self-critical, return again to critique their own methods and conclusions. This is how it should be, and indeed, always has been. I look forward to seeing what the future holds.

Further Reading

ROBERT B. STEWART

This brief bibliography is written by an involved nonspecialist in the field of New Testament studies and is intended to help readers who are also nonspecialists. I have tried to limit it to English-language translations. Most of the time I merely summarize the contents, but at times I offer some personal opinions. They are just that, my own opinions.

In the first section below, a year for the first edition in the language of origin may be added if it is different from the edition or translation recommended.

Classics of the Quest

Bousset, Wilhelm. *Kyrios Christos: A History of Belief in Christ from the Beginnings of Christianity to Irenaeus*. 1913. Translated by John E. Steely. Nashville: Abingdon Press, 1970.

Classic representative of the history-of-religions school (*religionsgeschichtliche Schule*), according to which the New Testament in general and the Synoptic Gospels in particular are but one part of a much larger sociohistorical phenomenon: the evolution of Jesus from Jewish Son of Man to Gentile God-Man.

Bultmann, Rudolf. *The History of the Synoptic Tradition*. 1921. Translated by John Marsh. Oxford: Basil Blackwell, 1963.

Vitally important book that rightfully recognizes the importance of understanding the nature of what was being taught about Jesus during the period between Jesus and the written Gospels. In so doing he goes a long way toward justifying form criticism and especially the criterion of dissimilarity. Sadly, in my view, this work shows that Bultmann misunderstood its primary subject.

——. *Jesus and the Word*. 1934. Translated by Louise Pettibone Smith and Ermie Huntress Lantero. New York: Scribner, 1958.

Bultmann's mature position on the relationship of Jesus to the Christian church and Christian orthodoxy. He is highly skeptical of recovering the historical message of Jesus because "the early Christian sources show no interest in either [his life or his personality], are moreover fragmentary and often legendary[,] and other sources about Jesus do not exist."

———. *New Testament and Mythology: And Other Basic Writings*. 1941–61. Selected, edited, and translated by Schubert M. Ogden. Philadelphia: Fortress Press, 1984.

This collection contains some of his most important essays, including "New Testament and Mythology," "Is Exegesis without Presuppositions Possible?," and earlier and later versions of "On the Problem of Demythologizing."

Harnack, Adolf. *What Is Christianity?* 1899–1900. London: Williams & Norgate, 1901.

In a good example of classic liberal Christology, Harnack argues that Jesus emphasized the imminent arrival of the kingdom of God, the fatherhood of God, the infinite value of the human soul, and the moral responsibility to keep the Great Commandment.

Kähler, Martin. *The So-Called Historical Jesus and the Historic, Biblical Christ*. 1892. Translated, edited, and introduced by Carl E. Braaten. Philadelphia: Fortress Press, 1964.

Questions the capacity of critical methods to reproduce Jesus. Notes that the historical Jesus is not the Christ whom the church worships. Concludes that the project of writing a biography of Jesus is doomed to failure and unnecessary as well.

Käsemann, Ernst. *Essays on New Testament Themes*. SBT 41. London: SCM Press, 1964.

Contains the 1954 paper that launched the New Quest, "The Problem of the Historical Jesus."

Reimarus, Hermann Samuel. *Reimarus: Fragments*. 1774–78. Edited by Charles H. Talbert. Translated by Ralph S. Fraser. Lives of Jesus Series, edited by Leander Keck. Philadelphia: Fortress Press, 1970.

Generally this book is the starting point in surveys of the Quest. It can be fairly described as conspiratorial in some sense and significantly influenced by deism.

Renan, Ernst. *La Vie de Jesus*. Paris: Michel Lévy Frères, 1863.

The first modern biography of Jesus. Like many of his time, Renan thought that Jesus was very non-Jewish in his character, values, and message.

Robinson, James M. *A New Quest of the Historical Jesus and Other Essays*. London: SCM Press, 1959. Reprint, Philadelphia: Fortress, 1983.

Robinson was the historian of the New Quest. This book is a good introduction to the "New Quest."

Schweitzer, Albert. *The Mystery of the Kingdom of God: The Secret of Jesus' Messiahship and Passion*. 1901. Translated by Walter Lowrie. New York: Macmillan, 1950.

Far less well known than Schweitzer's later book, this is his attempt to state briefly who Jesus really was. According to Schweitzer, Jesus was an apocalyptic prophet/messiah who mistakenly proclaimed the imminent end of the world. Ironically, it was published on the same day as Wrede's *Messianic Secret*.

———. *The Quest of the Historical Jesus: A Critical Study of Its Progress from Reimarus to Wrede*. 1906. Translated by W. Montgomery. New York: Macmillan, 1968. Reprint, Baltimore: Johns Hopkins University Press, 1998.

The book that (wrongly) is thought by many to have ended the Quest. Insightful at times; always written in stunning prose. One of the truly influential books in twentieth-century theology and New Testament studies.

Strauss, David Friedrich. *The Life of Jesus Critically Examined*. 1835–36. Edited by Peter C. Hodgson. Translated by George Eliot from the fourth German edition, 1840. Lives of Jesus Series, edited by Leander E. Keck. Philadelphia: Fortress Press, 1972.

Strauss wrote four books on Jesus. The first edition of this book has been the most significant because in it Strauss was the first to write that myth rather than history better captures the essence of Jesus' message. Influenced by Hegelianism, he criticized the rationalism of J. G. Herder and H. E. G. Paulus. He lost his job as a result. If he had written seventy years later, he would have become a celebrity rather than a pariah.

Troeltsch, Ernst. *Religion in History*. Translated by James Luther Adams and Walter F. Bense. Minneapolis: Fortress Press, 1991. Esp. pages 11–32.

Contains several essays by one of the most significant thinkers in the philosophy of history, including the 1898 "Historical and Dogmatic Method in Theology," in which Troeltsch lays out his three historiographical principles: (1) methodological doubt, (2) analogy, and (3) correlation.

Wrede, William. *The Messianic Secret: Forming a Contribution Also to the Understanding of Mark*. 1901. Translated by J. C. G. Greig. Cambridge: James Clarke, 1971.

Like Schweitzer, Wrede is highly critical of the earlier research on Jesus, believing it to suffer from "psychological suppositionitis," which makes Jesus so malleable that he can be anything to anyone. Insisting that Jesus never claimed to be Messiah, he infers that the messianic themes in the Gospels are the theological creation of the early church. His thesis has been hugely influential with many since then.

Surveys of the Quest / Introductions to the Quest

Beilby, James K., and Paul Rhodes Eddy, eds. *The Historical Jesus: Five Views*. Downers Grove, IL: InterVarsity Press, 2009.

Fine introductory summary of Jesus research to date (not too long, not too short), given by Robert Price, John Dominic Crossan, Luke Timothy Johnson, James D. G. Dunn, and Darrell Bock. Each presents his position, the other four respond, then the original presenter concludes. The format is typical of multiple-views books, but the content is superb.

Brown, Colin. *Jesus in European Protestant Thought, 1778–1860*. SHT 1. Durham, UK: Labyrinth, 1985.

Brown, a philosopher by profession, makes some quite interesting observations about the influences, motivations, and results of the Quest. Definitely not an average survey.

Charlesworth, James H. *The Historical Jesus: An Essential Guide.* Nashville: Abingdon Press, 2008.

One of Abingdon's "essential guides" intended for the interested layperson or student. Judicious choice of chapter topics and questions answered. One drawback is lack of footnotes. Brief and clear.

Dunn, James D. G., and Scot McKnight, eds. *The Historical Jesus in Recent Research.* Sources for Biblical and Theological Study 10. Winona Lake, IN: Eisenbrauns, 2005.

Everything the title says that it is and more. This impressive anthology contains recent—and not-so-recent—readings from familiar and not-so-familiar names. Excellent collection.

Neill, Stephen, and Tom Wright. *The Interpretation of the New Testament, 1861–1986.* 2nd ed. Oxford: Oxford University Press, 1988.

An insightful and entertaining survey and critique of 125 years of New Testament criticism. N. T. Wright updated it by writing the final chapter. One of the most important books of its kind.

Powell, Mark Allan. *Jesus as a Figure in History: How Modern Historians View the Man from Galilee.* 2nd ed. Louisville, KY: Westminster John Knox Press, 2013.

Helpful introduction to contemporary studies. Especially helpful summaries of the Jesus Seminar and of Crossan, Borg, Sanders, Meier, and Wright.

Strimple, Robert B. *The Modern Search for the Real Jesus: An Introduction to the Historical Roots of Gospels Criticism.* Phillipsburg, NJ: P&R Publishing, 1995.

Short but rich; especially helpful in understanding the philosophical issues related to the history of the Quest. Limited in terms of range, however, in that it stops at the New Quest, which is now old news. Would love to see it updated.

Tatum, W. Barnes. *In Quest of Jesus: A Guidebook.* 2nd ed. Nashville: Abingdon Press, 1999.

Helpful, basic book and exceptionally clear.

Theissen, Gerd, and Annette Merz. *The Historical Jesus: A Comprehensive Guide.* Translated by John Bowden. Minneapolis: Fortress Press, 1996.

Wide-ranging, well-informed, well-organized, and quite useful book; especially valuable as a sourcebook.

Weaver, Walter P. *The Historical Jesus in the Twentieth Century, 1900–1950.* Harrisburg, PA: Trinity Press International, 1999.

Massively informative book about how much was being done and by whom in the Quest when—according to some caricatures of First Quest, No Quest, New Quest—nothing was happening. Chronicles the Jesus research in France, Britain, and North America as well as Roman Catholic Jesus research in the first half of the twentieth century.

Books on Historical Reliability

Blomberg, Craig L. *The Historical Reliability of the New Testament: Countering the Challenges to Evangelical Christian Beliefs.* B&H Studies in Christian Apologetics. Nashville: B&H Academic, 2016.

The best case presently available for the historical reliability of the New Testament.

Cowan, Steven B., and Terry L. Wilder, eds. *In Defense of the Bible: A Comprehensive Apologetic for the Authority of Scripture.* Nashville: B&H Academic, 2013.

Solid scholarship from a team of conservative evangelicals, dealing with a wide range of issues related to biblical reliability. Particularly useful for the opening section on philosophical issues relating to historical reliability.

Habermas, Gary R., and Michael R. Licona. *The Case for the Resurrection of Jesus.* Grand Rapids: Kregel, 2004.

A "minimal facts" argument for the historicity of the resurrection of Jesus. "Minimal facts" are established by more-than-adequate scholarly evidence, leading the vast majority of contemporary scholars in relevant fields to acknowledge the historicity of the occurrence.

Licona, Michael R. *The Resurrection of Jesus: A New Historiographical Approach.* Downers Grove, IL: InterVarsity Press, 2010.

States and applies a new method that tests various hypotheses concerning Jesus' resurrection by assessing them as to their explanatory scope, explanatory power, plausibility, degree of ad hoc reasoning, and illumination. Licona makes a strong case for the historicity of the resurrection.

———. *Why Are There Differences in the Gospels? What We Can Learn from Ancient Biography*. Oxford: Oxford University Press, 2016.

Based on an exhaustive study of Plutarch, Licona argues that ancient biographers allowed for invention that was consistent with the message of the historical figure in focus in each biography. Applies this to the New Testament Gospels to explain some differences.

Wilkens, Michael, Craig Evans, Darrell Bock, and Andreas Köstenberger. *The Holman Apologetics Commentary on the Bible: The Gospels and Acts*. Nashville: B&H Academic, 2013.

Interesting book that goes through the New Testament Gospels to address spots where apologetic issues may arise. Each author covers an individual Gospel.

Third Quest / Recent Research of Interest

Crossan, John Dominic. *The Historical Jesus: The Life of a Mediterranean Jewish Peasant*. San Francisco: Harper & Row, 1991.

Pictures Jesus as a Jewish cynic. Much good background on the ancient Mediterranean world. Interesting and esoteric stratification of sources. Few would agree with his treatment of *Gospel of Thomas* or the *Gospel of Peter*, but many would listen and learn.

Crossley, James G. *The Date of Mark's Gospel*. London: T&T Clark International, 2004.

From a secular New Testament scholar, an impressive monograph that challenges the status quo concerning the dating of the Synoptic Gospels; suggests the Gospel of Mark could date as early as the late 1930s.

Dunn, James D. G. *Jesus Remembered*. Vol. 1 of *Christianity in the Making*. Grand Rapids: Wm. B. Eerdmans Publishing Co., 2003.

Dunn argues that the remembered Jesus, meaning the impression Jesus made on his followers, is the only Jesus to which historians have access. He claims that the remembered Jesus is to a significant degree consistent with the New Testament Gospels, when read through critical realist lenses.

Keith, Chris, and Anthony Le Donne, eds. *Jesus, Criteria, and the Demise of Authenticity.* New York: T&T Clark, 2012.

Quite significant book. Has the potential to change how Jesus research is done. Excellent scholars offer good articles on how to assess historical authenticity in Jesus research.

Le Donne, Anthony. *The Historiographical Jesus: Memory, Typology, and the Son of David.* Waco, TX: Baylor University Press, 2009.

Thoughtful and well-informed book, building on Dunn. Le Donne argues that the only Jesus is the remembered Jesus and that the remembered Jesus is always an interpreted Jesus. Eschewing historical positivism and critiquing Bultmann and his descendants, Le Donne offers a new way forward.

Wright, N. T. *Jesus and the Victory of God.* Vol. 2 of *Christian Origins and the Question of God.* Minneapolis: Fortress Press, 1996.

Impressive prose coupled with worldview analysis to show how Jesus was prophet, Jewish Messiah, and embodiment of YHWH.

———. *The Resurrection of the Son of God.* Vol. 3 of *Christian Origins and the Question of God.* Minneapolis: Fortress Press, 2003.

Around 600 pages of background showing that resurrection was widely understood to be bodily rather than metaphorical or "spiritual." Then comes a solid case for resurrection being the most plausible explanation for the mutation of Jewish resurrection belief that one finds among the earliest Christians.

Collections

Anderson, Paul N., Felix Just, and Tom Thatcher, eds. *Aspects of Historicity in the Fourth Gospel.* Vol. 2 of *John, Jesus, and History.* Atlanta: Society of Biblical Literature, 2009.

———, eds. *Critical Appraisals of Critical Views.* Vol. 1 of *John, Jesus, and History.* Atlanta: Society of Biblical Literature, 2007.

———, eds. *Glimpses of Jesus through the Johannine Lens*. Vol. 3 of *John, Jesus, and History*. Atlanta: Society of Biblical Literature, 2016.

These three impressive volumes feature top scholars demonstrating what Johannine scholarship has to offer Jesus studies. A long overdue contribution.

Bock, Darrell L., and Robert L. Webb, eds. *Key Events in the Life of the Historical Jesus: A Collaborative Exploration of Context and Coherence*. Grand Rapids: Wm. B. Eerdmans Publishing Co., 2010.

As a team of scholars, members of the Institute for Biblical Research report on their research concerning twelve supposed events in the life of Jesus; they do this after presenting their findings to one another and receiving critical feedback. An example of solid scholarship being improved through collaboration and constructive criticism.

Charlesworth, James H., and Petr Pokorný, eds. *Jesus Research: An International Perspective*. The First Princeton-Prague Symposium on Jesus Research. Grand Rapids: Wm. B. Eerdmans Publishing Co., 2009.

———, eds. *Jesus Research: New Methodologies and Perceptions*. The Second Princeton-Prague Symposium on Jesus Research. Grand Rapids: Wm. B. Eerdmans Publishing Co., 2014.

Both these volumes from Charlesworth and Pokorný feature impressive collections of essays delivered to one another by top international scholars, some conservative, some not. A good way to assess the current state of the field.

Evans, Craig A. *Fabricating Jesus: How Modern Scholars Distort the Gospels*. Downers Grove, IL: InterVarsity Press, 2008.

Useful popular-level book that addresses everything from conspiratorial novels like *The Da Vinci Code* to the noncanonical Gospels of *Thomas*, *Judas*, and *Peter*. Deals with the Cynic Jesus theory and other questions from lay readers.

Holmén, Tom, and Stanley E. Porter, eds. *Handbook for the Study of the Historical Jesus*. 4 vols. Leiden: Brill, 2011.

Massive collection (over 3,000 pages in 4 volumes) of fresh essays by a world-class group of scholars of all perspectives. The price is exorbitant.

Miscellaneous

Carter, Warren, and Amy-Jill Levine. *The New Testament: Methods and Meaning*. Nashville: Abingdon, 2013.

Intended as an introduction to the New Testament, this book not only describes what readers will find in each book but also explains the critical methods used to discover the historical and cultural background of each book, and finally how different readers in various times and places with different agendas have interpreted the text. The part on interpretation will be seen either as its greatest and most unique contribution or its most controversial component, depending on the reader.

Ehrman, Bart D. *Did Jesus Exist? The Historical Argument for Jesus of Nazareth*. San Francisco: HarperOne, 2012.

Pointed refutation of the conspiracy theory masked as an academic investigation that Jesus never existed. Whether one agrees with his conclusions or not, Ehrman is always honest, informative, and interesting.

———. *How Jesus Became God: The Exaltation of a Jewish Preacher from Galilee*. San Francisco: HarperOne, 2014.

With an essentially adoptionist Christology, Ehrman argues that Jesus became "God" in the same way as many others before him and after him in the ancient Mediterranean world.

———. *Jesus, Interrupted: Revealing the Hidden Contradictions in the Bible (and Why We Don't Know about Them)*. San Francisco: HarperOne, 2009.

The book that birthed this book.

———. *Misquoting Jesus: The Story behind Who Changed the Bible and Why*. San Francisco: HarperOne, 2005.

Entertaining and frequently informative book. Argues that we can't have confidence about the current New Testament because of intentional and unintentional corruption of the text as ancient scribes copied its books.

Haines-Eitzen, Kim. *The Gendered Palimpsest: Women, Writing, and Representation in Early Christianity*. New York: Oxford University Press, 2012.

Continues the discussion begun in her earlier book, giving evidence of how women were involved in the transmission of the New Testament books. It also shows how women were reading ancient Christian texts.

———. *Guardians of Letters: Literacy, Power, and the Transmission of Early Christian Literature.* New York: Oxford University Press, 2000.

Discusses the significant relationship between power and literacy in the ancient world as well as highlighting the role of female scribes. Addresses significant issues in New Testament textual criticism, thus broadening our understanding of church history.

Harnack, Adolf. *Date of the Acts and the Synoptic Gospels.* Translated by J. R. Wilkinson. New York: G. P. Putnam's Sons, 1911.

As far as I know, the first book that argues for an early date for the Gospels. Stronger than Robinson's in my opinion.

Levine, Amy-Jill. *The Misunderstood Jew: The Church and the Scandal of the Jewish Jesus.* San Francisco: HarperOne, 2009.

Intended for both Christians and Jews, this book is mostly directed toward Christians in order to clear away unhelpful, and sometimes even harmful, ideas about Jews, whether in the first century or the twenty-first century. A useful book for both groups in better understanding the other.

Robinson, John A. T. *Redating the New Testament.* London: SCM Press, 1976.

The most influential book that argues for an early date for the Gospels.

Index

abductive reasoning, 6
antiquity, 22, 43n27, 48, 49n39, 62
   with its different approach to history, 22, 52, 59
   and pedagogy, 48
   writing practices during, 35, 40–42
apocryphal Gospels, 40, 44, 46, 57, 58, 91
archaeological evidence of Gospels' authenticity, 35, 44–46, 67
autographs, 38–39, 42–43, 57

bias, 16, 17, 34, 51
Bible
   Leviticus
      chapter 12: 28
   Matthew
      chapter 1: 24, 27
      chapter 9: 25
      chapter 11: 58
      chapter 12: 79
      chapter 13: 52
      chapter 19: 79
      chapter 26: 26
   Mark
      chapter 2: 79
      chapter 5: 25
      chapter 10: 79
      chapter 13: 80
      chapter 14: 26
      chapter 15: 32
      chapter 16: 38
   Luke
      chapter 2: 28
      chapter 3: 27
      chapter 6: 79
      chapters 10–18: 47
      chapter 23: 32–33
   John
      chapters 7–8: 38
      chapter 19: 30
   Acts
      chapter 2: 59
      chapter 3: 60

census of Roman Empire in Luke, 19
chreiai, 49–51. *See also* pedagogy in late antiquity
contradictions in the Gospels, 29, 34, 47n35, 55, 62, 68
criteria
   of clarity, 4–5, 49, 51
   of coherence, 5
   of comprehensiveness, 4–5
   of correlation (fit to data), 4–5
   of double similarity and dissimilarity, 10, 81n22, 85
   of embarrassment, 3–4
   of fruitfulness, 5
   for historians, 5
   for historical accuracy of sources, 67
   for historical Jesus studies, 10, 76n2, 78n12, 80–81
   of predictability, 5–6

criteria (*continued*)
　Sean Carroll's list of, 4–5
　of simplicity, 4–5
cynicism, 9

Dead Sea Scrolls, 44–45, 58
discrepancies in the Gospels, 33, 36, 55, 56, 59, 60, 62, 64, 66, 67
　compared to Roman biographies of Otho, 50–51
　genealogies of Joseph, 27–28
　Jesus' birth, 28–30
　Jesus' crucifixion, 32–33
　Jesus' death, 30–31
　Jesus' healing of Jairus's daughter, 25–26
　Jesus' resurrection, 31
　as only apparent but not real, 46–48
　Peter's betrayal foretold, 26–27

epistemic methodism vs. particularism, 14
errors in texts, 12, 23, 34, 39, 42
evidence, 5, 6, 8–12, 18, 26, 35, 37n8, 39n15, 40–42, 44, 57, 67
　within documents, 36, 41–44
　giving rise to reevaluation, 84
　as occasional as regards history, 10
　of women involved in transmission of New Testament, 94
eyewitness testimony, 38, 39n15, 45, 48n37, 67, 72, 73, 83
　as memory, 77–78. *See also* memory

genre, 13, 50n42, 52, 63–64, 68–69, 73, 81
　of the Gospel of John, 59
　as determinative for understanding texts, 60–61

Harnack, Adolf von, 75, 79, 80, 86, 94
history, 1, 52, 62, 67, 83
　of antiquity, 40n19
　as derivative, 3
　as difficult but worthwhile, 19
　as distinct from a mirror or videotape, 59, 63, 66
　as distinguished from truth, 68–69, 73–74. *See also* truth
　and inferences, 2
　influenced by agendas, 3–4
　as interpretative, 2, 59
　as a matter of perspective, 4
　as never comprehensive, 3
　oral tradition as, 82n26. *See also* tradition, oral
　as portrait of the past, 35, 51–52, 57, 59, 60, 62–64
　like practicing medicine, 17
　as public discipline, 5
　as retelling past events, 1
　like science (chart), 7
　like scientific investigation, 4–5
　works of, 34–36, 38–39
historical criticism, 8–9
historical Jesus, 19, 21–23, 33–35, 53–55, 57–59, 70, 80–81, 84
　able to be found using sources, 67
　may not look like us, 10
　as the memorable Jesus, 52n47
　as the remembered Jesus, 77
　state of the quest for, 75
　will never be the real Jesus, 8
histories (examples from antiquity), 36–37
horizontal reading of the Gospels, 24–26, 31, 46, 47n35, 61–62, 66

INDEX

inerrancy, 16n18, 23, 26, 46
  different than historical reliability, 12–13
intention (of texts), 2, 13, 49, 62, 71

Josephus, 16, 45, 46, 71

Life of Christ in Stereo, 27, 66
Livy, 36, 38, 54

manuscripts, 18, 35–43, 54, 57
memory, 36, 48, 52n47, 53n48, 77, 78n12, 91
  as retaining the gist of an event, 78, 83
  See also eyewitness testimony, as memory
models, 4
  as heuristically helpful, 7–9
  for the historical Jesus, 8
  for reading Gospels as history, 9–12
multiple attestation, 54, 58

naturalism, 10–11
natural theology, 11

oral history, *see* tradition, oral
Oxyrhynchus, 40–41

Palestine, 44–45, 49n38, 53n48, 58, 61–62, 73
papyri, 35, 37, 39n16, 40, 43. *See also* manuscripts
parables as true but not historical, 68–69, 74
pedagogy in late antiquity, 48–49, 51, 60. *See also chreiai*
  allowed for editing and paraphrasing of events, 47–52, 66
  unlike modern practices, 52

philosophical influences behind quest for historical Jesus, 76
Plutarch, 50, 51, 90
presuppositions, 9, 10, 11, 82

Q (source), 50

reliability (of historical texts), 9, 12–14, 16–19, 22, 50n43, 78n12, 83, 90
remembered Jesus, 77, 91
resurrection, 2, 12, 19n21, 24, 31, 90, 92

Schweitzer, Albert, 8, 75, 76, 87, 88
science, 4–7, 9
  likened to history (chart), 7
skepticism, 39n16, 78n12, 82n26
  Descartes', 14n16
  historians should be skeptical about, 9
  thoroughgoing, 76
  toward the Gospels, 18
sources for history, 3, 34–35, 39, 52, 55, 58, 67, 70, 88, 91
  ancient, 29, 39, 44, 63–64
  for the Gospels, 16n18, 50
  the Gospels as, 18, 46, 53, 71, 79, 81, 86
Suetonius, 50n43, 51
Synoptic Gospels, 35, 48n37, 50n42, 53n48, 78n12, 80, 81n24, 82–83, 85
  as having an early date, 38, 78–79, 91, 94, 95

Tacitus, 37, 38, 50, 51, 62
theology, 8, 35, 44
  as cause for bias, 8, 9, 47, 80
  as distinguished from history, 22, 31, 34, 55, 57, 59, 70–71, 73
  natural, 11

tradition, 45, 73–74
  early Christian, 48, 80
  as formal and informal, uncontrolled and controlled, 82–83
  Gospel, 78n12
  oral, 61–62, 81–84
trust, 12, 16–18, 22
  as distinct from knowledge, 54
  as to historical reliability, 21–22, 32–34, 54–55, 69–70
truth, 4, 5
  as aim of both history and science, 7
  as distinct from history, 68–69
  as sometimes less plausible than fiction, 6

verisimilitude, 35, 43–46, 54–55, 58–59

Word of God, 8, 68
Wrede, William, 8, 75, 76, 87, 88

Printed in Great Britain
by Amazon